Sensational
SCULPTED CAKES

First published in Great Britain 2016

Search Press Limited
Wellwood, North Farm Road,
Tunbridge Wells, Kent TN2 3DR

Illustrations and text copyright ©
Rose Macefield 2016

Photographs by Paul Bricknell at Search Press Studios

Photographs and design copyright ©
Search Press Ltd, 2016

ISBN: 978-1-78221-197-6

The Publishers and author can accept no responsibility for any consequences arising from the information, advice or instructions given in this publication.

Suppliers

If you have difficulty in obtaining any of the materials and equipment mentioned in this book, then please visit the Search Press website for details of suppliers:
www.searchpress.com

You are invited to visit the author's website:
www.rosemacefieldcakecraft.com

Printed in China

Dedication

To my husband, Kevin, as without his love, support and infinite encouragement, I would not have been able to write this book. To my wonderful children for their patience and my proud parents for their continued love and support.

Acknowledgements

Special thanks to my staff, who are extremely supportive and who worked hard to look after the business while I took time out to complete this work, and for all the encouragement they have given me along the way. Thanks also to the team at Search Press for all their help throughout the whole process and for making me feel at home during the photo shoots.

Sensational
SCULPTED CAKES
9 amazing designs to carve, shape and decorate

Rose Macefield

Search Press

CONTENTS

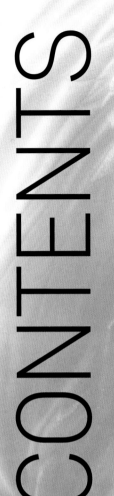

28

Best in Show

46

Rock 'n' Roll

56

Messy Monster

INTRODUCTION

I made my first cake when my son was christened in 2007, having always enjoyed art and craft. From then on I made every family cake. Later I enrolled in a cake decorating course at Wolverhampton College and completed with a distinction.

My hobby eventually developed into an exciting new business venture, Rose-Maries Cakes. As the business started to grow, I discovered cake shows and saw an opportunity to really challenge myself. I entered Cake International for the first time in 2009 with a figurine sculpture of Dobby the House Elf from Harry Potter, and I was delighted to win my first ever Bronze Award.

While my home-based business was doing well, I also had a desire to branch out and share my expertise. Already trained in teaching, I started offering cake decorating classes for beginners. They were very popular and I soon became keen to open up a cake shop and sugarcraft school. My first shop opened in 2011 and quickly outgrew the premises, so I moved to larger premises a year later.

I continued entering competitions and soon discovered I had a passion for cake carving and figure sculpting. In 2011 I won my first Gold Award. Over the next few years I won several Gold and Silver awards and then in 2013 I won Best in Show. Best of Best in show followed at the Cake Masters Awards in 2014.

I was invited to join the Cake International judges' team and I have judged at each competition since, which I thoroughly enjoy.

In 2015 I rebranded the business as Rose Macefield Cake Artist School of Sugarcraft, with the emphasis on teaching and writing projects. I had been writing regular step by step projects for magazines, and I was keen to write my own sculpted cakes book, as I love sharing my knowledge and experience with others.

The sculpted cakes in this book are for cake makers who are just beginning to sculpt cakes and also for the more advanced cake maker. The cakes have been designed to capture a realistic finish that will enable you to create head-turning cakes yourself. Each project will teach you how to create the essential support, carve the correct shape and proportions and cover the cake to achieve the best result. You will learn all the techniques required to apply the finishing touches to bring each cake to life with a realistic wow factor.

The projects feature a variety of themes including music, hobbies and sport, so there should be something for everyone. The step by step instructions mean you can create exactly the same cake for yourself, but I also encourage you to add your own personal touches to the designs, by changing colours or adding or removing some of the elements.

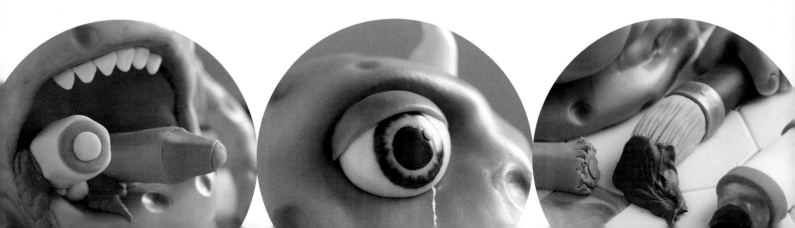

MATERIALS

Cake construction

Madeira cake

This is the most suitable cake base for cake sculpting as it is most important that the cake is firm enough to hold its shape while carving, but it must also be moist and tasty. While supports are often used in sculpted cakes, they will not hold up in a soft, delicate sponge cake. See the recipe for madeira cake on page 12.

Buttercream

Buttercream is used for filling and covering the cakes in preparation for covering with fondant (sugarpaste). It is quick and easy to make and easy to spread. See the recipe on page 13.

Royal icing

Royal icing is required for piping details onto cakes but can also be used for covering and creating a variety of textures. It is also a great material for gluing decorations onto cakes and for filling and repairing the fondant (suparpaste) covering. See the recipe on page 13.

Cake drums and cake cards

Cake cards are thin boards and are used for support within cakes. They are also handy for placing decorated items and cakes on while they are drying. They come in a variety of shapes and sizes and can be cut to size using a craft knife. The final cake is always displayed on a thicker cake drum.

Food-safe dowels and poly dowels

Traditional dowels are wooden or plastic, and are used for supporting cake tiers or for rolling out pastes to an even depth. Poly dowels are plastic and hollow. The red ones offer light support and the white ones are ideal for heavy support. They are used within cakes and decorations to offer stability to sculpted cakes. Cut the larger ones with a craft knife. The smaller ones can be cut with scissors.

Icing (powdered) sugar

This is used for rolling out fondant (sugarpaste) and is an essential ingredient for making buttercream and royal icing.

Cake covering

Fondant (sugarpaste)

Also referred to as roll-out icing, this is used for covering cakes and cake drums and for making modelled elements and decorations. It is available in white or a range of colours (and in chocolate flavour) and is sold by local and online sugarcraft stockists.

Modelling paste

Made by kneading Tylose (CMC) powder into fondant (sugarpaste) to make it firmer so that it holds its shape better when modelling and sets harder when dry. Use 1 tsp of powder to 500g (1lb 2oz) of paste. You can also buy ready-made modelling paste.

Chocolate chips

These can be added to the madeira cake and can also be used in decorations.

Marzipan

Used for covering cakes and a great medium to model with.

Flowerpaste

Also referred to as gum or petal paste, this is a firm paste that holds its shape well while drying. It dries very quickly and sets hard, and is ideal for making flowers, leaves and lettering.

Main tools

Most of these tools are used for making every cake project, so they are not included in the 'You will need' lists at the beginning of each project.

KNIVES A large cake knife is essential for carving cakes. A serrated edge is best. Small, sharp knives are used for delicate carving and for cutting fondant (sugarpaste). Palette knives are used for spreading buttercream and royal icing and the mini palette knife for trimming and cutting fondant (sugarpaste) and for picking up decorations. A craft knife is used for cutting large food-safe poly dowels.

CUTTERS AND PLUNGER CUTTERS A variety of these are used for adding decoration to cakes.

ROLLING PINS Used for rolling out fondant (sugarpaste).

PIPING BAG AND NOZZLES Used with royal icing for piping details onto cakes. A variety of nozzles can be used to achieve different effects.

WATER BRUSH This has a barrel that is filled with water, for gluing small items together.

SCISSORS Used for cutting out templates and cutting red poly dowels, and for creating texture in fondant (sugarpaste).

MODELLING TOOLS Used for creating texture and modelling. The Dresden tool creates sharp creases and fur textures; the stitching tool creates a stitched effect; the cone tool is for pointed indentations; the ball tool is for making holes and indentations and various other tools are used for adding decoration.

BRUSHES For dusting, gluing and painting.

SUGARCRAFT CLAY GUN This includes interchangeable discs to create a variety of fondant (sugarpaste) and marzipan decorations. Used often for making ropes and stands.

TAPE MEASURE For measuring cakes and decorations.

AIRBRUSH For colouring the finished cake and for creating stripes and patterns, woodgrain effects, stencilled patterns, shading and colour depth.

SMOOTHER For creating smooth finishes, keeping sides straight and rolling neat sausages of fondant (sugarpaste).

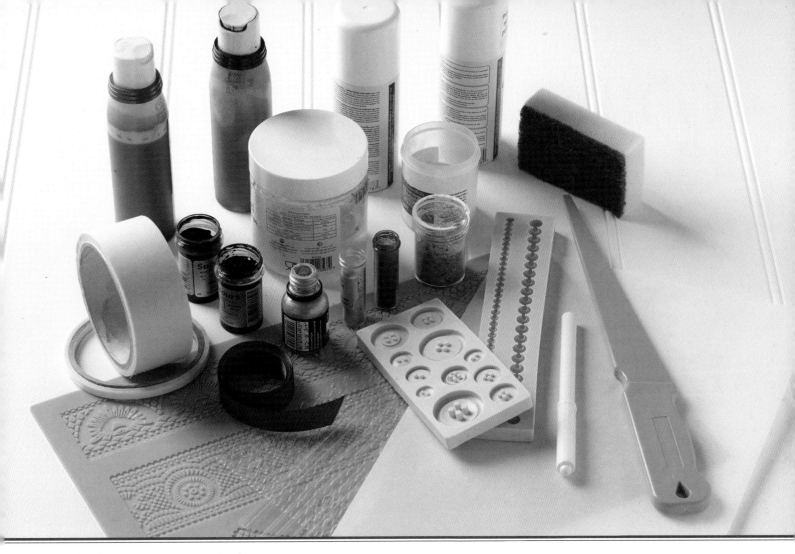

Other materials

MASKING TAPE For creating stripes and patterns when airbrushing.

EDIBLE PASTE COLOURS Food colouring pastes. Colour your own fondant (sugarpaste) and marzipan by kneading in small amounts.

EDIBLE DUSTS These can be applied lightly with a brush for adding shade, or mixed with clear alcohol for painting details.

METALLIC PAINTS Edible paints for creating a metallic effect.

AIRBRUSH COLOURS Suitable edible paint that can be mixed to create different colours.

EDIBLE SPRAY GLAZE Sprayed on cakes to give a slight sheen or a high shine. Spray in light coats and allow drying time between each application.

LUSTRE SPRAY Silver, pearl and black are sprayed on cakes to achieve a metallic or shining effect.

TYLOSE/CMC For adding to fondant (sugarpaste) to make a modelling paste. Also used for making glue.

PIPING GEL For creating a water/fluid effect. Used to make egg whites. Can also be used as glue.

SILVER GLITTER FLAKES For creating the silver specks on a black iced cake drum to resemble a granite worktop.

EDIBLE LACE MOULD AND KNIFE For creating edible lace with an edible lace mix. The lace is usually baked in the oven but can be air-dried overnight.

SILICONE MOULDS For making buttons and beads quickly and accurately.

EDIBLE PENS For marking small details.

EDIBLE WAFER PAPER Used for creating decorations to resemble wrappers.

RIBBON For decorating the edges of the cake drum.

DOUBLE-SIDED TAPE For attaching ribbon to cake drums.

SCOURER Used for creating a light grass impression.

Madeira cake

The recipe for Madeira cake that I use for sculpted cakes is shown below. This table shows you the amounts and baking times needed for round cakes from 13cm (5in) to 33cm (13in), and for square cakes from 10cm (4in) to 30cm (12in), so it should cover everything you need.

TIP

I usually adapt this recipe when I'm decorating regular cakes rather than sculpted cakes, by halving the amount of plain flour. This will give a moister, less dense cake.

Method

1   Preheat the oven to 160°C/325°F/Gas 3. Grease and line the base and sides of the cake tin.

2   Add the butter and caster sugar to the mixer and mix for approx. five minutes until light and pale.

3   Beat the eggs and add the flavouring. Gradually add the egg and some of the flour to the butter and caster sugar mix. Fold in the remaining flour.

4   Fill the tin and bake for the recommended time. Baking times can vary between ovens. To prevent a crust forming on the outside of the cake, wrap the tin with a couple of layers of newspaper (place it well away from the flame if using a gas oven). You can also place a sheet of baking parchment on the shelf above to help reduce the crusting on top.

5   When the cake is baked, it will be springy when pressed on top. You can also check by inserting a clean knife into the centre. The knife should come out clean.

Madeira cake recipe for sculpted cakes

Round	13cm (5in)	15cm (6in)	18cm(7in)	20in (8in)
Square	10cm (4in)	13cm (5in)	15cm (6in)	18cm (7in)
Butter (unsalted)	115g (4oz)	175g (6oz)	225g (8oz)	350g (12oz)
Caster sugar	115g(4oz)	175g (6oz)	225g (8oz)	350g (12oz)
Self-raising flour	115g (4oz)	175g (6oz)	225g(8oz)	350g (12oz)
Plain flour	50g (2oz)	75g (3oz)	125g (4½ oz)	175g (6oz)
Eggs (large)	2	3	4	6
Baking times	45min–1 hour	1–1¼ hours	1–1¼ hours	1¼ –1½ hours
(160°C/325°F/Gas 3)				

Flavourings (per 6 egg recipe):

vanilla or any other essence: 5ml.   Lemon: 2 grated rinds.   Coconut: 100g (3½oz) desiccated coconut.

Buttercream

Recipe

500g (1lb 2oz) unsalted butter at room temperature
1kg (2lb 3oz) icing (powdered) sugar

Method

Place the butter into the mixing bowl and whisk at low speed. Add the sugar gradually until the mixture is soft. Store in the fridge.

Royal icing

Recipe for a small amount

1 tsp of meri-white (dried albumen)
4 tsps of water
Sieved icing (powdered) sugar

Method

Mix the meri-white and water, then add the sugar gradually until it reaches the correct consistency. The correct consistency for royal icing is to form soft peaks in the mixture if you are piping lettering and small details or sticking things together. It should form stiff peaks if you are piping larger details. For the projects in this book, you need soft peak icing.

Recipe for 750g (10½oz)

42g (1½oz) of meri-white (dried albumen)
170ml of water
1.2kg (2lb 10oz) of icing sugar

Method

Mix the meri-white and water, then add as much of the sugar as is needed to achieve soft peak consistency (see left).

	23cm (9in)	25.5cm (10in)	28cm (11in)	30cm (12in)	33cm (13in)
	20in (8in)	23cm (9in)	25.5cm (10in)	28cm (11in)	30cm (12in)
	450g (1lb)	500g (1lb 2oz)	700g (1½ lb)	850g (1lb 14oz)	1kg (2¼ lb)
	450g(1lb)	500g (1lb 2oz)	700g (1½ lb)	850g (1lb 14oz)	1kg (2¼ lb)
	450g(1lb)	500g (1lb 2oz)	700g (1½ lb)	850g (1lb 14oz)	1kg (2¼ lb)
	225g (8oz)	250g (9oz)	350g (12oz)	425g (15oz)	500g (1lb 2oz)
	8	9	12	15	18
	1½–1¾ hours	1½–1¾ hours	1¾–2 hours	2–2¼ hours	2¼–2½ hours

Levelling, stacking and slicing through

Cakes are usually domed a little on the top when they are baked. It is necessary to level the cake before it is decorated, especially if the cake is going to be stacked. Stacking cakes is quite often required when sculpting. Slicing through the cake a couple of times allows you to add a filling to enhance the taste – in the projects in this book, I have used buttercream.

1

2

1   You can level cakes in the tins, or by measuring the height at the corners and scoring with a knife. Hold a ruler between the marks and slice off the top.

2   Stack the cakes as required. To improve the taste and moisture, you will need to slice through and add buttercream. Measure and score as for levelling, then slice through. Spread all the inside surfaces with buttercream.

Supporting cake stucture

Strong support

Use the large white food-safe poly dowels where more support is needed. Always mark the dowel flush with the top of the cake, then take it out, cut it to size with a craft knife and replace it. These step by step pictures are from the What's Baking? cake on page 100.

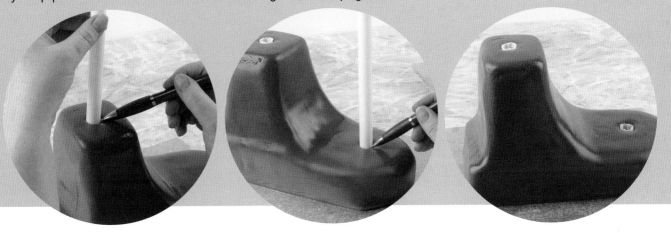

Extra support

Cake cards are often needed within cakes for extra support and you can also use the red poly dowels within the white ones. For this cake, the white dowel (pushed inside the cake) supports the circular cake card. I cut a hole in the board so that the red dowel fits inside. The red dowel and the board support the mixing bowl and hold it in place.

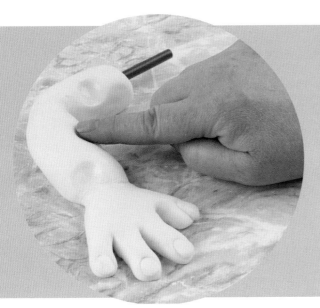

Supporting decorations

The red poly dowels are used for supporting small decorations. In the Messy Monster project (page 56), I have used them to help support the arms and keep them from breaking off.

Basic sculpting

Sculpting cake can be quite scary when you are a beginner but it is often easier than you think. When sculpting, I use templates and measurements, but you can also use photographs to guide you when carving freehand. You need sharp, serrated knives both for carving the main shapes and for shaving and cutting off small pieces until you achieve the required shape. If you accidently cut too much off, you can usually use a little buttercream to attach it back on.

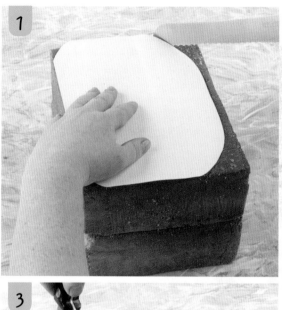

1 When using a template, score around the template first. This step shows me making the basket for the Catch of the Day cake (page 78).

2 Remove the template and cut out the shape, following the scored outline. To carve the side edges, hold the knife straight, at right angles to the work surface. In this step, I am carving the curved corners of the basket, removing the original cake's sharp corners.

3 When carving the top edges, hold the knife at an angle and shave off the sharp edges of the cake.

4 For a smooth, rounded finish, use a smaller knife to sculpt freehand, carefully shaving off any unwanted sharp edges. This step shows me carving the mixer shape for the What's Baking? cake on page 100.

Sculpting faces

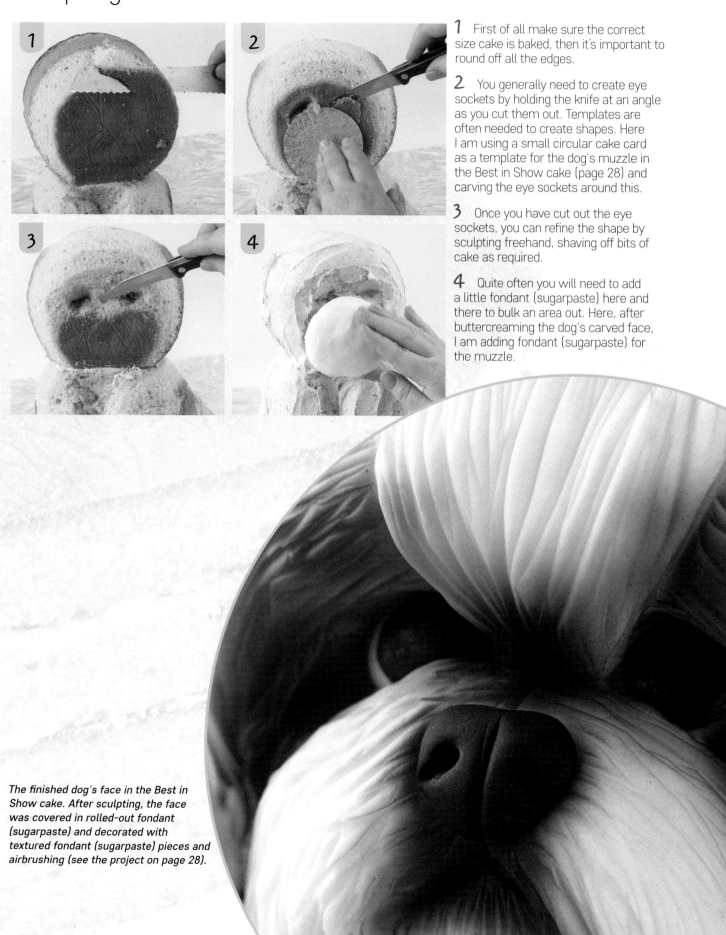

1 First of all make sure the correct size cake is baked, then it's important to round off all the edges.

2 You generally need to create eye sockets by holding the knife at an angle as you cut them out. Templates are often needed to create shapes. Here I am using a small circular cake card as a template for the dog's muzzle in the Best in Show cake (page 28) and carving the eye sockets around this.

3 Once you have cut out the eye sockets, you can refine the shape by sculpting freehand, shaving off bits of cake as required.

4 Quite often you will need to add a little fondant (sugarpaste) here and there to bulk an area out. Here, after buttercreaming the dog's carved face, I am adding fondant (sugarpaste) for the muzzle.

The finished dog's face in the Best in Show cake. After sculpting, the face was covered in rolled-out fondant (sugarpaste) and decorated with textured fondant (sugarpaste) pieces and airbrushing (see the project on page 28).

Using templates

1 When placing a template against the side of the cake, use dressmakers' pins to hold it in place. Always count how many you use so that you do not leave any in the cake. Score the outline first. Remove the template, count the pins to check you have removed them all and then pin the template to the other side of the stacked cakes, with all the elements facing in the same direction. Score again.

2 Remove the template, counting the pins again and and cut the shape, using the scored outline as a guide.

3 Round cake cards are ideal for using as templates for rounding off parts of your sculpted design.

4 For straight edges, you can use a square cake card as a template.

CAKE COVERING

Cakes are generally covered with fondant (sugarpaste) but you can also use marzipan, royal icing or buttercream.

Covering a cake drum

Covering the cake drum with fondant (sugarpaste) not only creates a professional finish, but is an important part of the design for a sculpted cake.

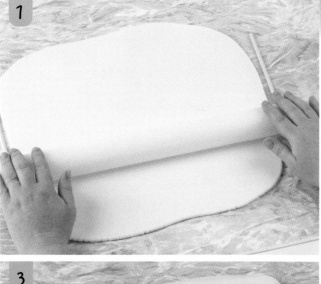

1 Sprinkle icing (powdered) sugar on your work surface and knead the fondant (sugarpaste), then roll it out, using dowels to ensure an even depth. Keep lifting the fondant (sugarpaste) and turning it round to prevent sticking.

3 Smooth the fondant (sugarpaste) with a smoother.

2 Lightly wet the cake drum with water using a brush. Lift the rolled-out fondant (sugarpaste) on the rolling pin and hold it over the cake drum.

4 Trim off the excess round the edges with a small palette knife.

Colouring fondant (sugarpaste)

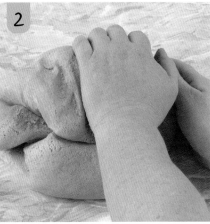

1 Here, I am colouring a large amount of fondant (sugarpaste) a chocolate colour, using chestnut and dark brown edible paste colours. Smear some of each colour on the fondant (sugarpaste).

2 Knead the colours through the paste, adding more as necessary, to achieve a chocolate brown.

Covering a sculpted cake

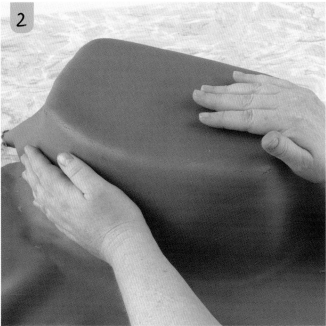

1 Roll out the fondant (sugarpaste) large enough to cover the total area, making sure to roll to 5mm (¼in) thickness. Use the rolling pin to lift the fondant (sugarpaste) over the buttercreamed cake.

2 Once the fondant (sugarpaste) is in place, work quickly with your hands to make sure the top edge is smoothed on. Work on the corners first, then gradually work down towards the bottom of the cake.

3 Use the cake smoother to make sure the fondant (sugarpaste) is smooth and tidy. Press the fondant (sugarpaste) closer to the board and use the edge of the smoother to score a line round the base of the cake, creating a cutting line.

4 Trim neatly around the cutting line using a palette knife and remove the excess fondant (sugarpaste).

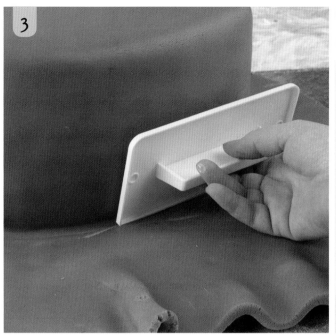

Joining pieces of fondant (sugarpaste)

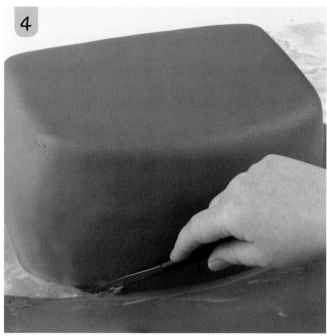

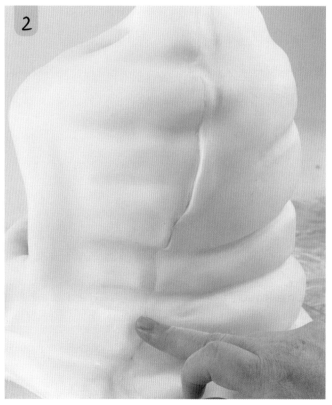

1 For tall sculpted cakes like the Messy Monster (page 56), you may need to cover the cake in sections and join the fondant (sugarpaste) together. Start by covering one half and trim a neat edge. Then cover the other half, overlapping the coverings. Trim with a palette knife through both layers as shown.

2 Brush water over the join and gently smooth the fondant (sugarpaste) with your finger until the join disappears.

A variety of techniques can be used with fondant (sugarpaste) to decorate sculpted cakes.

Marbling paste

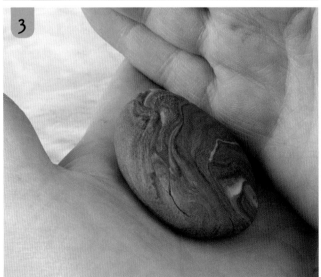

1 Take two pieces of fondant (sugarpaste).

2 Knead them together so that the colours begin to merge. Make sure you leave streaks of the separate colours, to create the marbled effect.

3 Roll into the shape required. This marbled paste was used to make pebbles in the Catch of the Day project. It also looks great rolled out flat to make floor tiles, as shown in the Teenage Kicks project (below, right) or plectrums for the Rock 'n' Roll guitar (below, left).

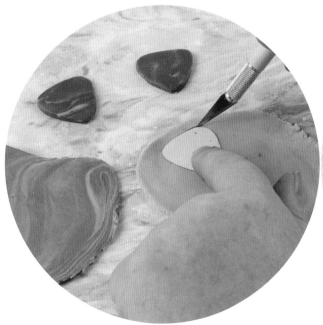

Using a clay gun to make strands

A clay gun will allow you to achieve a variety of decorations with speed and accuracy. It is particularly good for creating strands.

1 Put a little white vegetable fat in the clay gun first, then make a sausage from fondant (sugarpaste) and push it inside.

2 Use the correct attachment to make the type of strand you want. This shows the round attachment used for the basketweave effect of the Catch of the Day project (page 78). Squeeze out the strand.

3 For a professional finish, you can smooth the stand using the smoother as shown.

TIP
You can also make strands by rolling a long sausage and then neatening with a smoother.

Adding texture

Adding texture to fondant (sugarpaste) while it is still soft will allow you to enhance the design and achieve realistic results.

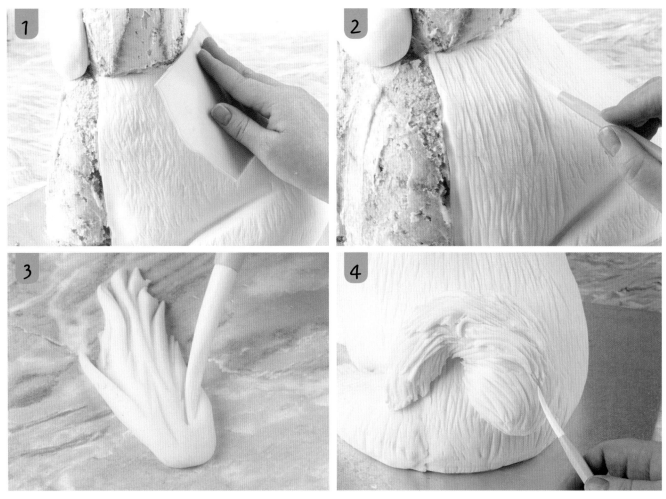

1 Texture the fondant (sugarpaste) first with a short fur texture mat.

3 To add further texture for a really fluffy look, make a tapered cone from a small amount of fondant (sugarpaste), then flatten and tuft this with the Dresden tool.

2 Vary and intensify the texture with the Dresden tool.

4 Stick onto the cake and repeat to make the surface even fluffier. This tuft is being added to the tail of the Best in Show dog. Continue adding tufts until you are happy with the result.

Other ways of adding texture

Right: Use a clean scouring pad, as in Anyone For Tennis? (page 90).

Far right: Metal mesh can also be used to create texture, as for the fish scales in Catch of the Day (page 78).

Airbrushing

An airbrush is a small air-operated nozzle and works with edible food colour to decorate a cake. Airbrushing your cakes allows you to blend colours, achieving a seamless finish, and can create a realistic look. The airbrush can create a variety of effects including woodgrain, shadowing and marbling. Patterns can also be created using stencils. Shown below is the airbrushing of the guitar in the Rock n' Roll cake (page 46).

1 Use the template to make a stencil and place it on top of the covered cake. Weigh it down with small coins or similar to prevent movement. If parts of the template are likely to lift during airbrushing, hold them down with the end of a paintbrush. Fill the bowl of the airbrush, in this case with red airbrush colour. Try it out on scrap paper first. Press the trigger gently to get an even flow of colour.

2 Spray the sides of the cake in the same way. Leave twenty minutes between coats to allow the paint to dry. You will need two or three coats to achieve the depth of colour shown.

3 Remove the template and spray yellow airbrush colour over the white parts. Allow to dry.

4 Spray red over the yellow to create a flame effect, making the colour deeper on the tips of the flames. Allow to dry.

5 Fill the airbrush with black. Spray close to the cake and very carfully to highlight the flames by applying black in the teardrop shapes between them.

Modelling basic shapes

When modelling you need to learn how to make basic shapes first. All the shapes start with a ball.

Ball Roll a piece of fondant (sugarpaste) between your hands to form the shape. It is harder than it looks to get a perfect ball shape. Used for eyes.

Teardrop Roll a ball between your hands to taper off the side of it. I used these for the dog's whiskers on the Best in Show cake (page 28).

Cone Taper off a ball but flatten the larger end. I used this shape to make the horns on the Messy Monster (page 56).

Disc Roll a ball and then flatten it. I used this shape to make the centre of the fishing rod reel for the Catch of the Day cake (page 78).

Cube Roll a ball and then flatten it between smoothers. I used this to make the building blocks for the Toy Train cake (page 112).

Mushroom Create the shape by rolling a ball then rolling half of it a bit more between your fingers.

I used this shape to make the drawer knobs on the craft box for the Get Crafty cake (page 124).

Sausage Roll fondant (sugarpaste) with your hands and then roll over it with a smoother to perfect it.

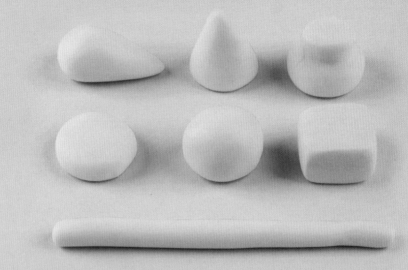

Top row, left to right: teardrop, cone, mushroom. Middle row: disc, ball, cube. Bottom: sausage.

Finishing touches

Spraying with edible spray glaze allows you to achieve a sheen or a glossy finish. Spray in fine coats, allowing each one to dry before the next. Apply just one coat for a sheen or several coats for a high gloss.

Spray with silver lustre spray to achieve a chrome or silver finish.

You can make paint by adding clear alcohol to edible paste colour. This creates bold colours.

Apply edible dusts with a paintbrush to achieve subtle finishes such as the make-up brush in the Teenage Kicks project (page 68).

Colour royal icing with edible paste colour and pipe it from a piping bag to achieve the spilt paint in the Messy Monster project (page 56).

I created the fish for the Catch of the Day cake (page 78) using a variety of finishing touches. I sprayed with silver, pearl and black lustre sprays for the main colour, then I dusted the faint pink line down the body and painted the spotty pattern with edible paste colour mixed with clear alcohol.

BEST IN SHOW

This cake is a popular with adults and children alike, as everyone thinks their precious pooch is 'best in show'! This is a shitzu, but the colours and facial features can be changed if you refer to photographs, so other breeds can be created too.

You will need

- Madeira cakes: one 25.4 x 17.8cm (10 x 7in), one 15cm (6in) square and one 15cm (6in) round
- 45.8cm (18in) circular cake drum
- Buttercream
- 10cm (4in) and 7.5cm (3in) circular cake cards
- Wide and narrow food-safe poly dowel
- 4.25kg (9lb 6oz) white fondant (sugarpaste)
- Short fur texture mat
- Edible paste colour in dark brown, black and green
- Clear alcohol such as vodka
- Clear edible spray glaze
- A little black fondant (sugarpaste)
- 300g (10½oz) white modelling paste
- Kitchen paper
- Mid-brown, dark brown and black airbrush colours
- 7.5cm (3in), 5.7cm (2¼in) 5cm (2in) and 2.5cm (1in) circle cutters
- Former e.g. apple tray section
- Edible silver lustre spray
- Icing ruler
- 100g (3½oz) red flowerpaste
- 50g (2oz) red modelling paste
- Letter tappit
- 60g (2oz) gold modelling paste
- Heart and circle plunger cutters
- Pawprint silicone mould
- Small amount of royal icing (see page 13)
- Silver ribbon
- Double-sided tape
- Large piping nozzle

1 Level the rectangular and square cakes, place the square on top of the rectangle, then slice through and spread with buttercream (see page 13). Place a 10cm (4in) circular cake card on top as a sculpting guide.

2 Round off the top with the large knife to create shoulders.

3 Hold the knife vertically, with the tip on the work surface, and carve off the corners.

4 Carve away more of the front to create a more rounded shape.

5 Carve the back end off at an angle as shown.

6 Flip the offcut over so that it creates the dog's back and rear as shown. Fix into place with buttercream.

7 Use a smaller knife to carve a 'Y' shape at the front, below the round cake card. Angle the knife to avoid cutting too deeply. Shave away at the cuts to create the shape between the dog's front legs.

8 Use the large knife at an angle to taper the bottom of the cake all the way round. Measure 7.5cm (3in) round from the front of a leg and carve out a line. Carve into this recess to sculpt the shape of the leg. Repeat for the other leg.

9 Round off the back of the dog, shaving off any rough or hard edges.

10 Score a line for the haunch and carve into this to shape the back leg. Taper the body leading up to it to emphasise the haunch. Repeat the other side.

11 Refine the shape, arching the back a little more and shaving off any hard cake edges, for instance at the fronts of the legs. Keep shaving off until you are happy with the shape.

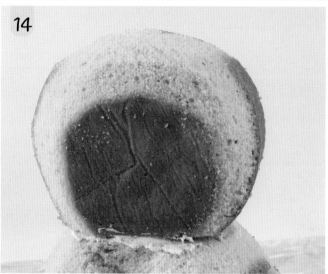

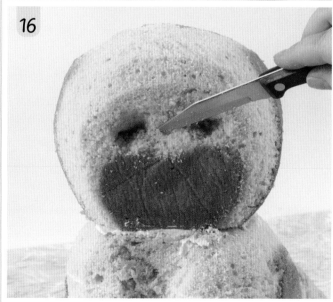

12 Cut a piece of food-safe poly dowel to 23cm (9in). Remove the circular cake card from the top of the cake and push in the dowel, down to the work surface.

13 Do not level the round cake. Cut off one edge as shown, then place it on the dowel for the head with a circular face to the front. Carve away the round cake's edges to round off the shape.

14 When you are happy with the overall shape, stick the head on with buttercream.

15 Hold a 7.5cm (3in) circular cake card against the face as shown, and carve out two eye sockets just above it with a medium knife.

16 Carve out and soften the edges of the eyes sockets.

33

17 Place the cake on a board and coat it all over in buttercream. Shape 100g (3½oz) of fondant (sugarpaste) into a ball, flatten it and stick it to the front of the face, just below the eyes, to form the muzzle.

18 Knead and roll out 1.5kg (3lb 5oz) fondant (sugarpaste) to 5mm (¼in) thick. Drape it over the dog's body using the rolling pin.

19 Smooth it into the dog's shape with your hands, then trim off at the neck with a small knife.

20 Push the fondant (sugarpaste) under at the bottom with the Dresden tool, then trim off.

21 Reinforce the shape of the haunches using the Dresden tool, then smooth it with your fingers.

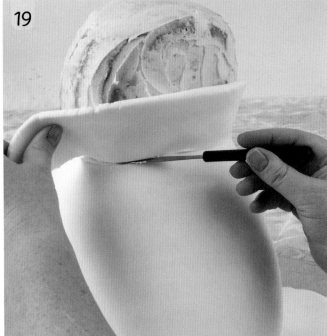

22 Texture with a short fur texture mat.

23 Vary and intensify the texture with the Dresden tool.

24 Roll 100g (3½oz) of fondant (sugarpaste) into a tapered sausage and shape the front into a paw. Wet the haunch and press on the leg. Blend the leg into the haunch with water and the Dresden tool, then texture it with the texture mat and Dresden tool as for the body.

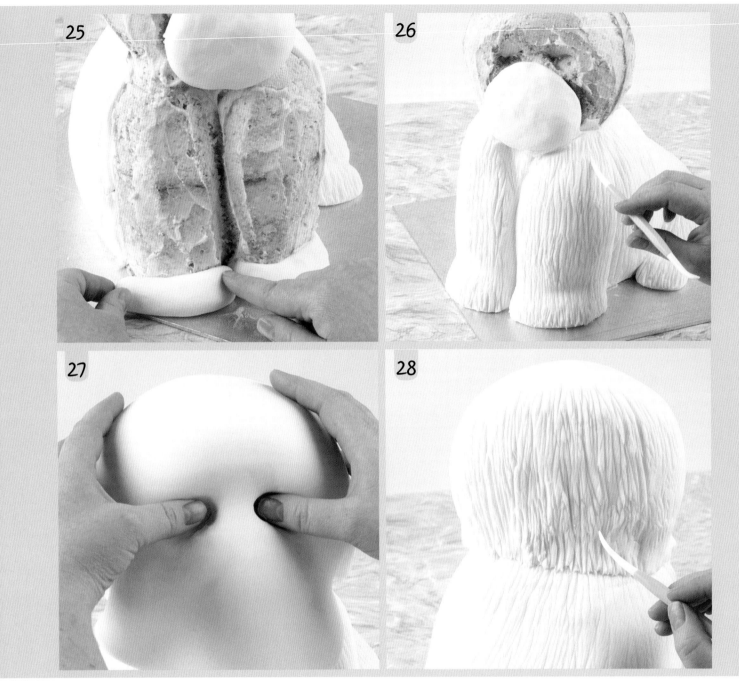

25 Make fat sausages of fondant (sugarpaste) to bulk out the front paws and stick them on. Brush on a little water.

26 Roll out 1.5kg (3lb 5oz) of fondant (sugarpaste) for the front of the dog as for the back, and drape it over, smooth and trim it as before. Texture with the texture mat and Dresden tool.

27 Roll out 500g (1lb 2oz) of fondant (sugarpaste) in the same way to cover the head. Push in the eye sockets with your thumbs. It doesn't matter if this tears the fondant (sugarpaste), as you will be adding eyes.

28 Trim the head covering at the back with a knife. Texture with the texture mat and Dresden tool.

29 Shape the fondant (sugarpaste) round the muzzle and trim off at the bottom with a small knife.

30 Use the Dresden tool, and then your fingers, to shape the mouth in an upside-down 'V'.

31 Shape two balls of fondant (sugarpaste) into ovals 2.5cm (1in) across. Offer them up to the eye sockets to check that they fit, and reshape them accordingly. Paint the irises with dark brown edible paste colour mixed with a little clear alcohol. Allow to dry, then paint the pupils with black edible paste colour. Glaze with clear edible spray glaze.

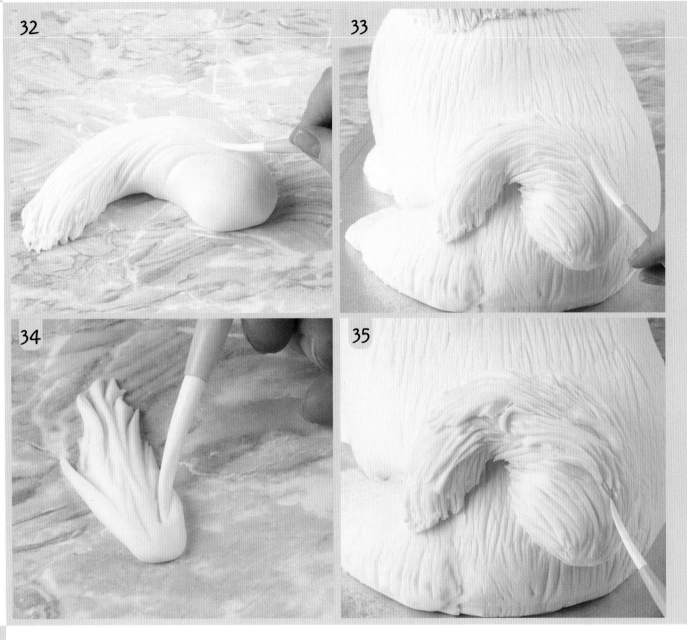

32 Shape 200g (7oz) of fondant (sugarpaste) into a tapered sausage, flatten it a little and curve to form a tail. Texture roughly with a Dresden tool.

34 Make a tapered cone from a small amount of fondant (sugarpaste), then flatten and tuft this with the Dresden tool.

33 Wet the dog's rump and stick on the tail. Blend and texture with the Dresden tool, drawing out the fondant (sugarpaste) into tufts.

35 Stick onto the tail and repeat to make the tail fluffier. Continue adding tufts until you are happy with the result.

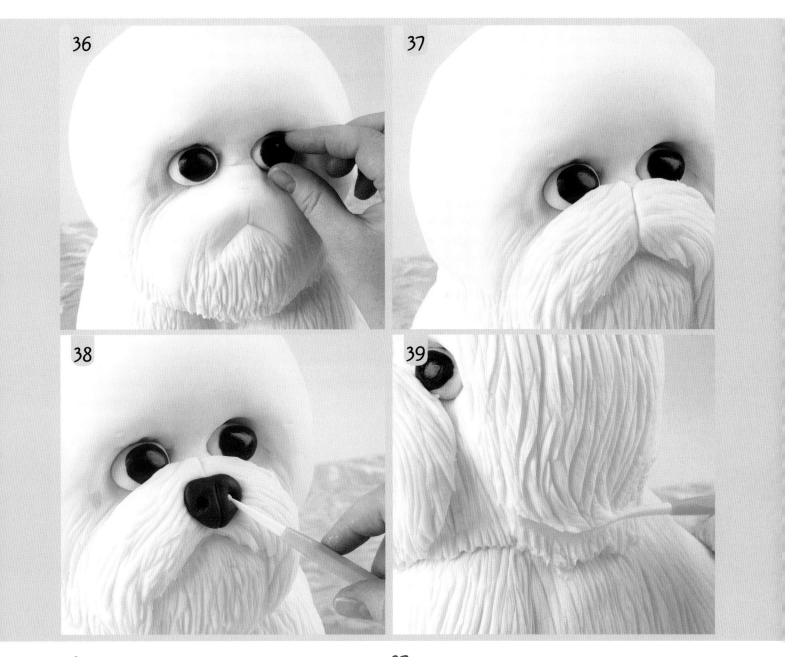

36 Wet the eye sockets and place the eyes. You might need to reshape the sockets to fit.

38 Push in a little dent for the nose to sit in. Roll a ball of black fondant (sugarpaste) 1.8cm (¾in) across. Shape it into a flattened triangle with curved edges and press it on, using water to stick it in place. Make a line down the centre with the Dresden tool, then use the ball tool to make nostrils.

37 Make two flattened sausages from 70g (2½oz) fondant (sugarpaste) for the moustache. Texture and tuft as for the tail. Offer up to the dog's muzzle to try for size, then stick on. Blend and texture the moustache pieces into place.

39 Take 175g (6oz) white fondant (sugarpaste) for each ear. Roll out oval shapes around 17.8cm (7in) long. Texture with the texture mat, then stick on with water and texture and blend in place. Put in a few waves with the Dresden tool to show that the hair is long. To create tufts, use the Dresden tool to push icing out and texture the edges.

40   Cut out a wide centre parting by removing the top part of each ear where they meet on top of the head. Roll out 70g (2½oz) fondant (sugarpaste) 7.5cm (3in) square and place this piece in the parting. Texture it to suggest hair being drawn up into the topknot in front.

41   Take 150g (5¼oz) of white fondant (sugarpaste) for this and the next two steps. Make tufts from small amounts fondant (sugarpaste) as in step 34 and place below each eye as shown.

42   Make each eyebrow from a tapered sausage flattened into a curved oval 10cm (4in) long and 5cm (2in) wide at one end. Texture as before and place as shown.

43   Roll out a triangle of fondant (sugarpaste) around 9 x 7cm (3½ x 2¾in). Place it as shown from between the eyes to the hair parting, like hair gathered into a topknot. Texture as before.

44   To make the tuft on top, make a flattened bean shape 7.5cm (3in) long and 5cm (2in) wide in the middle, from 50g (1¾oz) of modelling paste. Texture it on both sides with the Dresden tool to show hair fanning out as shown. Stick it in place, supporting it with your fingers. Separate some of the strands with the tool. You may need to place a ball of kitchen paper behind the tuft as it dries.

45 Mix mid-brown airbrush colour with alcohol to make it paler, and test it out on paper. Angle the airbrush to go round the dog's eyes but not in them and press gently on the trigger to get a precise flow of colour.

46 Hold your hand behind the tuft of the topknot and spray the edges only.

47 Airbrush the ears and the back of the head and body, leaving patches white as shown.

48 Complete the base coat as shown. Leave to dry for twenty minutes between coats.

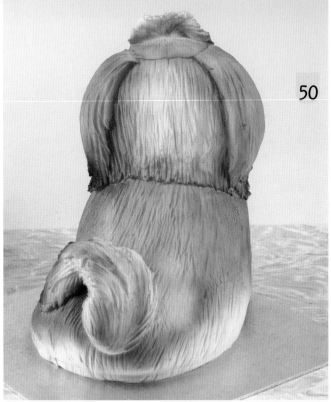

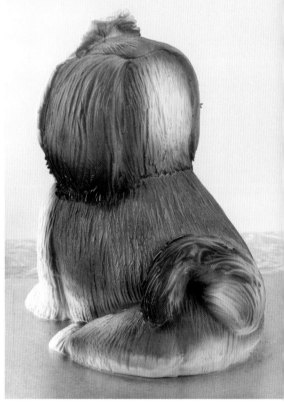

49 Make a darker brown with dark brown and black mixed in a ratio of 10 to 1 drops. Spray round the eyes and the base of the ears, using kitchen paper as a mask where needed. Continue spraying over the base colour to deepen the tone.

50 This shows the back with the deeper tone applied.

51 Mix a warm, redder mid-brown and apply a coat all over the base coat, leaving patches as before. Add more black and enhance the darker tones round the base of the ears, eyes and tail. Airbrush round the nose and mouth, and then spray the nose itself.

52 Finally, spray a light brown between the dog's legs. He can now go on the cake drum covered with 1.25kg (2lb 12oz) fondant (sugarpaste) coloured with green edible paste colour.

The back of the dog with the airbrushing finished.

53 Take 125g (4½oz) of white modelling paste, mould it into a ball, flatten it and use a 7.5cm (3in) circle cutter to cut out a deep circle as shown. Use a small palette knife to cut off angles to make an octagonal base for the trophy.

54 Make the circular parts to go on top in the same way but without cutting off to make angles. Use a 5cm (2in) and a 2.5cm (1in) cutter and stack the layers as shown. Wet an 8cm (3¹⁄₈in) piece of narrow food-safe poly dowel, and feed a sausage of modelling paste to half-way up. Smooth between your hands, then trim the paste to 4cm (1½in). Push the dowel down into the trophy as shown.

55 For the cup part of the trophy, mould 150g (5¼oz) of modelling paste into a ball and cut off a bit for the handle. Flatten the bottom and use a rolling pin to hollow it out. Trim the top with scissors to flatten it.

56 Put the cup in a former; I used a section from an apple tray. Make sausages of modelling paste 9cm (3½in) long and 8mm (¼in) thick, cut the ends and curve as shown for the handles. Leave all the pieces to dry overnight. Stick them together with a little royal icing and spray with edible silver lustre spray.

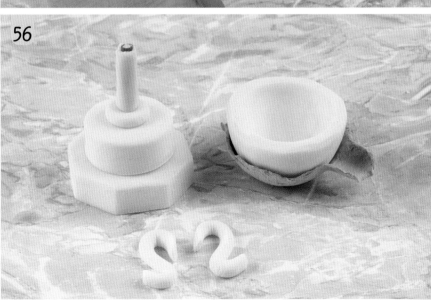

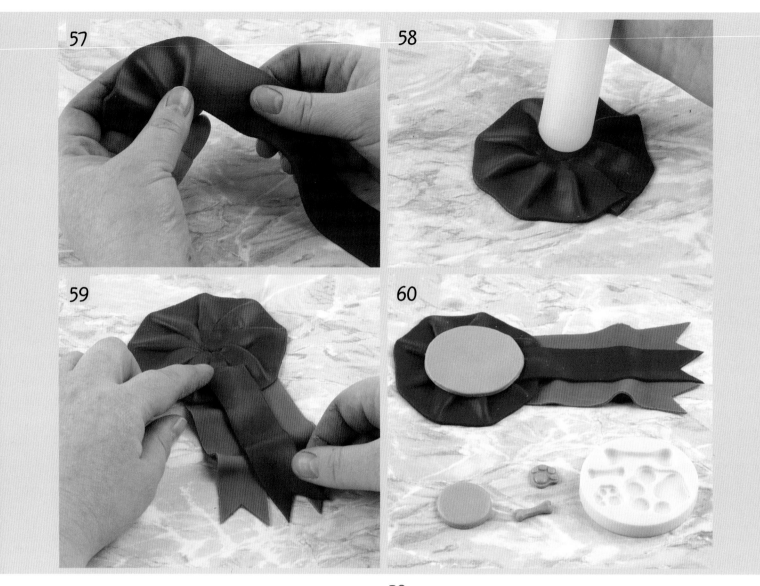

57 Roll out 60g (2oz) red flowerpaste thinly for the rosette. Cut it into a 30.5cm (12in) strip using a ruler. Make a little pleat, turn and pleat again as shown, until you have a full circle.

59 Use an icing ruler to make a narrower ribbon in red flowerpaste, 2.5 x 12.7cm (1 x 5in). Now cut two ribbons the same size from red modelling paste, which is a paler colour. Cut V shapes in the bottom of all three. Attach the lighter ribbons to the back of the rosette and the flowerpaste one on top. Assemble with waves in the ribbon as shown.

58 Push a rolling pin end into the middle to preserve the shape. Flatten with a smoother.

60 Roll out 50g (1¾oz) of gold modelling paste 3mm (¹/₈in) thick and use a 5.7cm (2¼in) circle cutter and a large piping nozzle to cut out circles. Stick the larger one to the rosette. Use the pawprint silicone mould to create a pawprint and small bone.

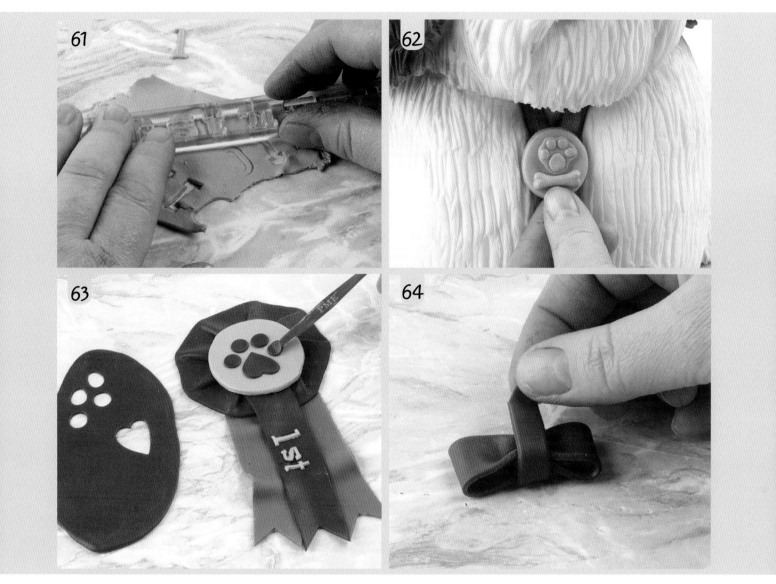

61 Use the letter tappit to make '1st' from a little thinly rolled gold modelling paste.

63 Cut a 2cm (¾in) wide heart with a plunger cutter and four circles, brush them with water and assemble on the rosette to make a pawprint.

62 Roll out a little red flowerpaste and cut two ribbons 4 x 1.5cm (1½ x ½in). Stick these under the dog's chin, assemble the medal as shown and stick it to the ribbons.

64 Make a ribbon for the dog's topknot by making a loop from a strip of red flowerpaste, then a band to go over the middle. Arrange all the pieces and trim the cake drum with silver ribbon, attaching it using double-sided tape.

ROCK 'N' ROLL

This cake is perfect for the budding rock star! Guitarists and rock lovers alike will love it. It is a good project for someone who is just learning to carve, as it is not too challenging, but it has the wow factor.

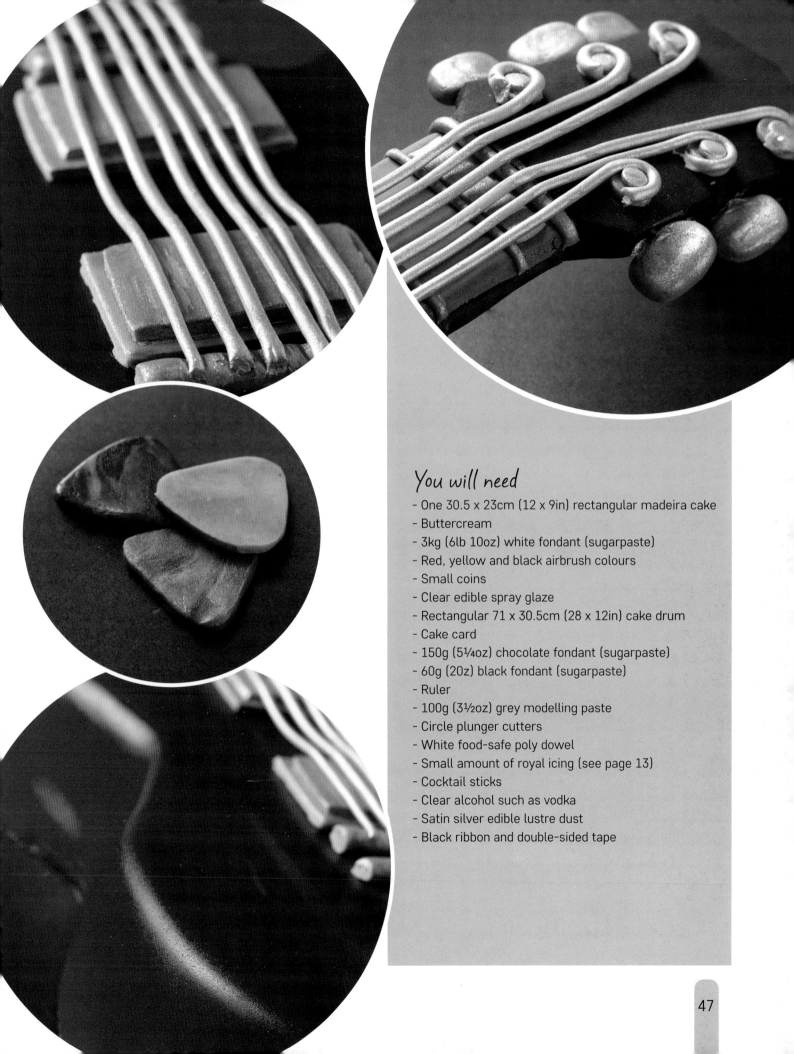

You will need

- One 30.5 x 23cm (12 x 9in) rectangular madeira cake
- Buttercream
- 3kg (6lb 10oz) white fondant (sugarpaste)
- Red, yellow and black airbrush colours
- Small coins
- Clear edible spray glaze
- Rectangular 71 x 30.5cm (28 x 12in) cake drum
- Cake card
- 150g (5¼oz) chocolate fondant (sugarpaste)
- 60g (2oz) black fondant (sugarpaste)
- Ruler
- 100g (3½oz) grey modelling paste
- Circle plunger cutters
- White food-safe poly dowel
- Small amount of royal icing (see page 13)
- Cocktail sticks
- Clear alcohol such as vodka
- Satin silver edible lustre dust
- Black ribbon and double-sided tape

1   Level the top of the cake, cutting its height down to 5cm (2in). Put the template for the main body of the guitar (see page 136) on top and score then cut around it.

3   Put the flame template (page 137) on top and weigh down with items such as small coins so that it does not move. You may need to hold the tips of the template down using a paintbrush handle while you airbrush the cake. Fill the airbrush bowl with red airbrush colour and spray the top red.

2   Buttercream the cake carefully, avoiding damaging the cake, as you need good, sharp edges. Roll out the fondant (sugarpaste) 4mm ($^3/_{16}$in) thick and cover the cake. Push and smooth into the recesses, being careful to avoid splitting. Shape the edges with a smoother. Trim the edges and tuck under using the Dresden tool. Neaten with the smoother. Allow the fondant (sugarpaste) to dry overnight.

4   Spray the sides. You will need several coats to achieve the desirable depth of colour. Allow twenty minutes drying time in between coats.

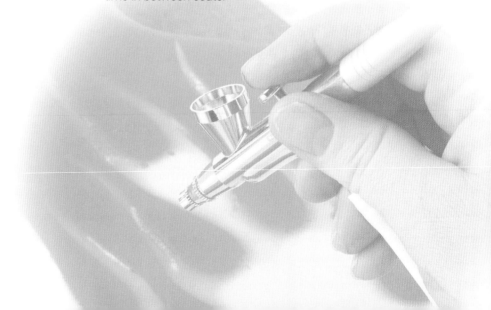

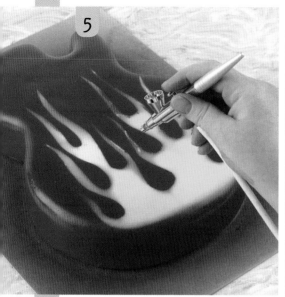

5 Remove the template and airbrush the white parts yellow.

6 Use red again to airbrush over the tips of the flames to create an orange glow.

7 Change the airbrush colour to black and spray carefully in the shapes between the flames to highlight them. Leave the airbrushing to dry, then glaze the cake with clear edible spray glaze.

8 Cover the cake drum with white fondant (sugarpaste). Airbrush from the edges inwards to create a graded effect, slightly lighter in the middle. Allow to dry, then go back round the board several times, leaving twenty minutes between each coat.

9 To make the guitar's neck, cut a 38 x 4.5cm (15 x 1¾in) rectangle from a cake card then trim so it tapers to 3.8cm (1½in) at one end. Make a mark 7.5cm (3in) from the narrow end. Bend the neck at this point.

10 Turn the card over and brush it with a little water. Roll out 150g (5¼oz) of chocolate fondant (sugarpaste) into a strip and cover the neck from the bend to 5cm (2in) from the wider end. Trim neatly at the ends and sides with a small palette knife.

11 Mix 100g (3½oz) of white fondant (sugarpaste) with a little of the chocolate fondant (sugarpaste) and roll it into a long strip. Stick it to the other side of the guitar neck, leaving just the head (beyond the bend) free. Trim it and push it down to meet the darker brown, covering the cut edge of the card. Allow to dry for a day.

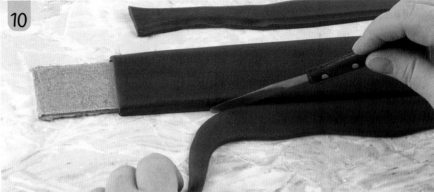

12 Roll out 60g (2oz) of black fondant (sugarpaste) and use the guitar head template (page 136) to cut out the shape twice.

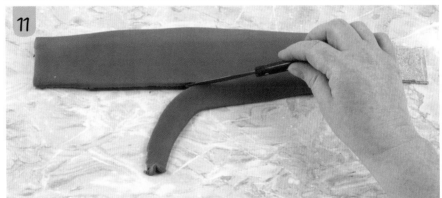

13 Dampen the cake card and stick one to the front and one to the back to make the guitar head.

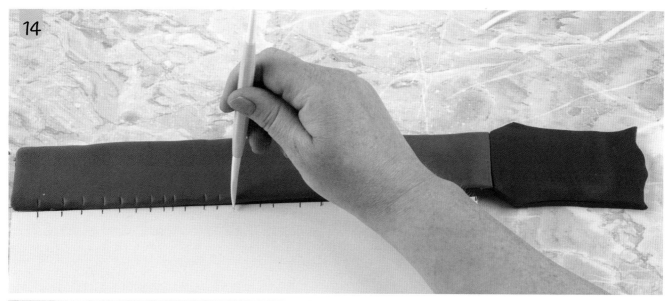

14 Use the template on page 136 to mark the frets and score the lines with a Dresden tool and ruler.

15 Roll out a long sausage 2mm ($^1/_{16}$in) thick from 30g (1oz) of grey modelling paste. Brush the scored lines with water and place the frets. Trim them where the neck front meets the darker paste behind.

16 Cut wide white poly dowel into lengths of 5.5cm (2¼in) and 3.5cm (1³⁄₈in) and cover them with black fondant (sugarpaste).

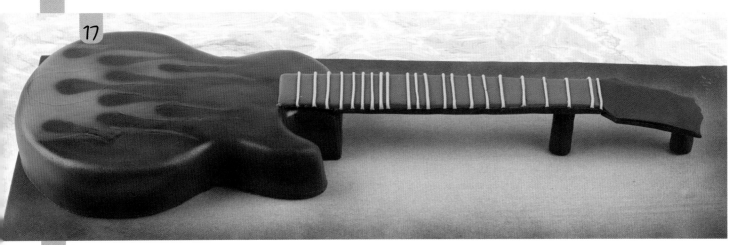

17 Place the guitar on the airbrushed cake drum. Lean the wide end of the neck on the guitar body as shown, and attach with a little royal icing. Place the longer support under the other end of the neck and the shorter one under the head, with a little royal icing to attach them.

18 Roll a thin sausage 4.5cm (1¼in) long from grey modelling paste and use water to attach it to the end of the guitar neck. Use a smoother to neaten it.

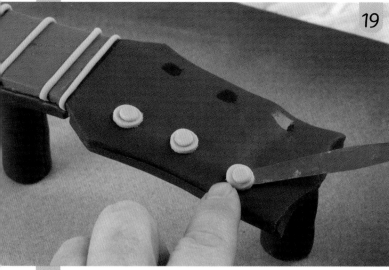

ADDING DETAILS

19 Roll out grey modelling paste and use the two smallest circle plunger cutters to create the screws in the guitar head where the strings attach. Dampen the paste and stick them in place as shown.

20 Make little balls and flatten them to make oval-shaped keys. Break off bits of cocktail stick 2.5cm (1in) long and use these to attach the keys.

21 Make position markers for between the frets by rolling out grey modelling paste. Cut nine plaques, three 1cm (³⁄₈in) wide and six 0.5cm (¼in) wide; all 3.5cm (1³⁄₈in) long. Brush with water and stick in position as shown.

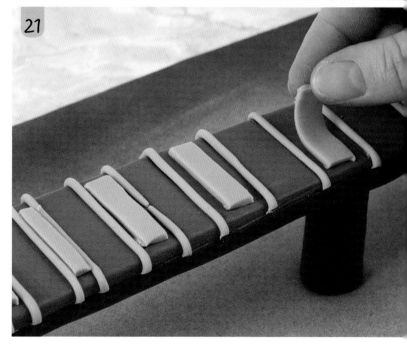

21

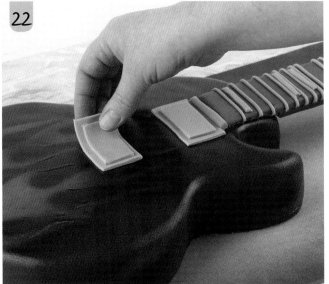

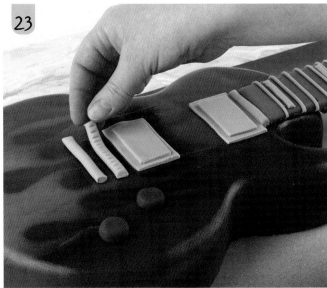

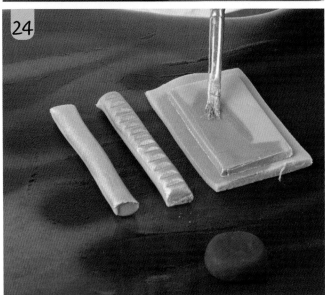

22 Make two plaques to go on the body of the guitar. Roll out grey modelling paste and cut two rectangles 5 x 2.5cm (2 x 1in) and two 6 x 3cm (2⅜ x 1¼in). Stick the smaller ones to the larger ones with water and stick to the guitar as shown, again brushing with water first.

23 Roll two small balls of black fondant (sugarpaste), flatten them into discs 1.5cm (⅝in) across and stick to the guitar as knobs. Make two sausages of grey modelling paste for where the strings attach, 6 x 0.5cm (2⅜ x ¼in). Flatten both and use the Dresden tool to cut grooves for the strings in one strip. Stick them on as shown.

24 Paint all the grey details silver using satin silver edible lustre dust mixed with clear alcohol.

25 Make the strings with grey fondant (sugarpaste). You can do this with a clay gun as shown, or roll a long, very thin sausage, neatening it with a smoother. They should be 51cm (20in) long.

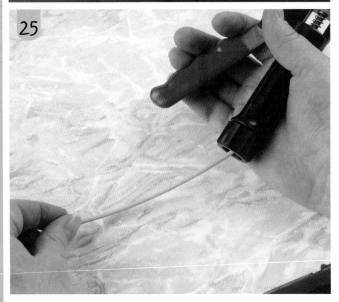

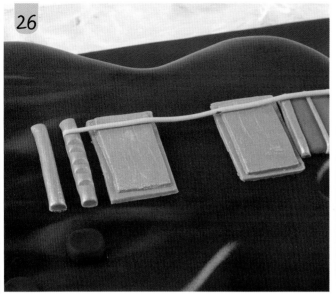

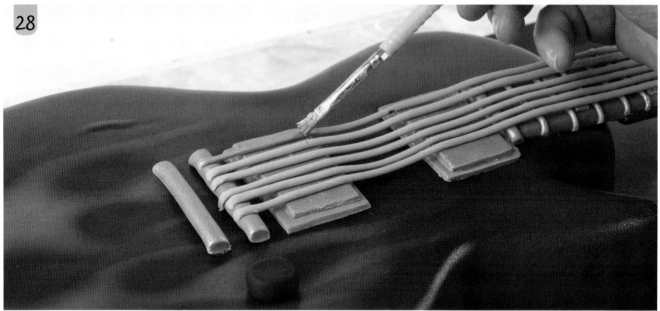

26 Place the strings as shown, beginning from the grooved strip.

27 Take the string to the head end, loop it round a screw and trim.

28 Paint the strings with the silver mix as before.

29 To make plectrums, marble together bright colours of fondant (sugarpaste). Roll out and use the template on page 136 to cut out the shapes. Smooth the edges with your fingers for a realistic look. Arrange them on the cake drum with the guitar. Trim the edge of the cake drum with black ribbon, attached using double-sided tape.

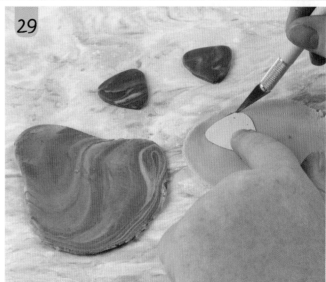

MESSY MONSTER

The perfect cake for the messy person in your life!
I have made several monster cakes for customers
and they always create a great reaction. You can
really get creative by changing the colours and
decorations. Why not make a greedy, sporty,
happy, grumpy, sleepy or pretty monster
instead? The shape may seem tricky
to carve but it really doesn't matter
as monsters can be any shape!

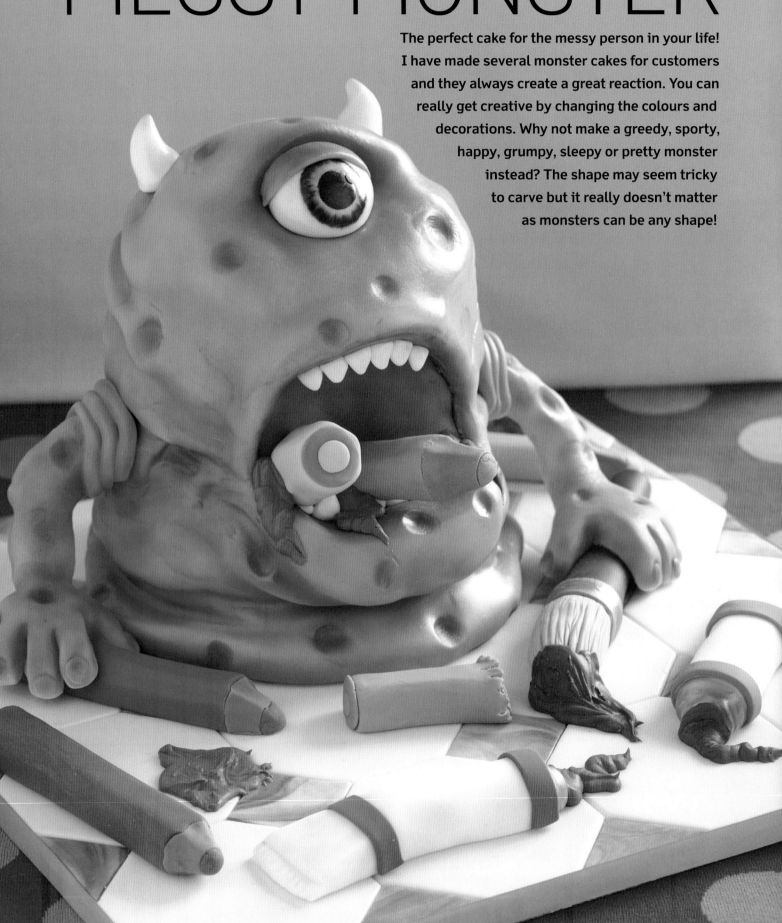

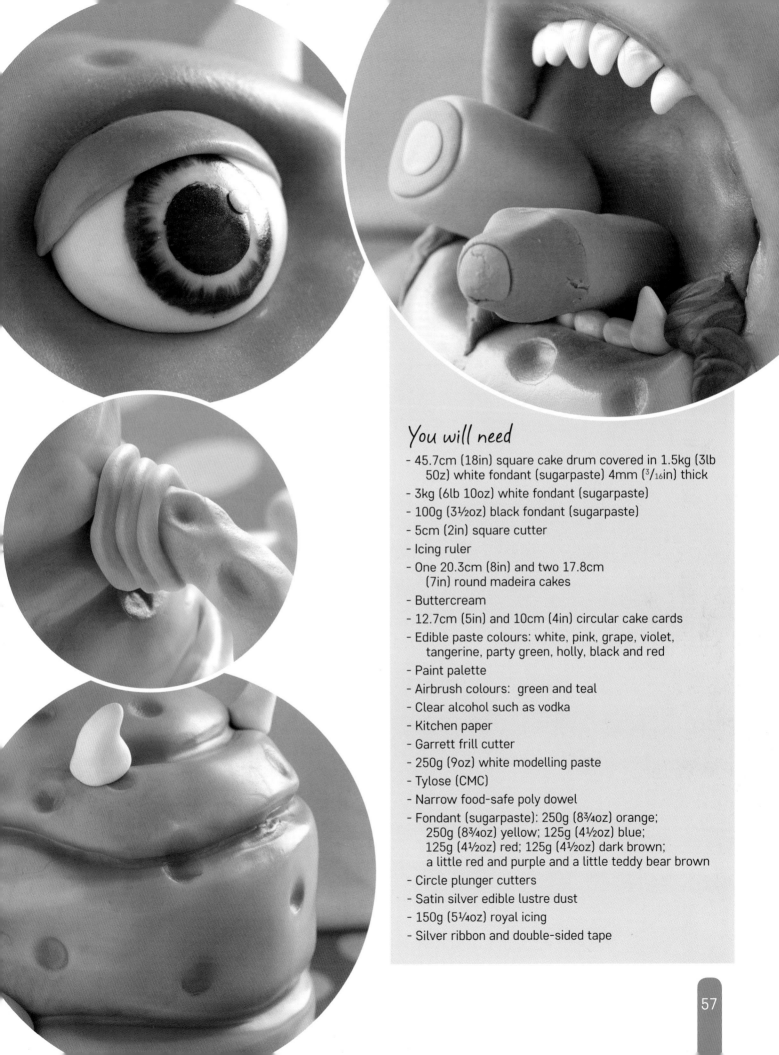

You will need

- 45.7cm (18in) square cake drum covered in 1.5kg (3lb 50z) white fondant (sugarpaste) 4mm ($^3/_{16}$in) thick
- 3kg (6lb 10oz) white fondant (sugarpaste)
- 100g (3½oz) black fondant (sugarpaste)
- 5cm (2in) square cutter
- Icing ruler
- One 20.3cm (8in) and two 17.8cm (7in) round madeira cakes
- Buttercream
- 12.7cm (5in) and 10cm (4in) circular cake cards
- Edible paste colours: white, pink, grape, violet, tangerine, party green, holly, black and red
- Paint palette
- Airbrush colours: green and teal
- Clear alcohol such as vodka
- Kitchen paper
- Garrett frill cutter
- 250g (9oz) white modelling paste
- Tylose (CMC)
- Narrow food-safe poly dowel
- Fondant (sugarpaste): 250g (8¾oz) orange; 250g (8¾oz) yellow; 125g (4½oz) blue; 125g (4½oz) red; 125g (4½oz) dark brown; a little red and purple and a little teddy bear brown
- Circle plunger cutters
- Satin silver edible lustre dust
- 150g (5¼oz) royal icing
- Silver ribbon and double-sided tape

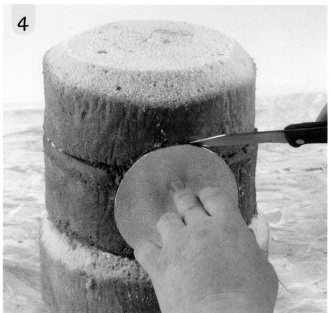

1 Mark the iced cake drum at 11.5cm (4½in) intervals and score with an icing ruler and the Dresden tool to make rows of four floor tiles. Use a 5cm (2in) square cutter to take out smaller tile shapes on the diagonal.

2 Marble black and white fondant (sugarpaste), roll it out to 3mm (³/₁₆in) thick and cut squares to stick in the holes. Trim off the edge ones.

3 Level the cakes, slice and buttercream them and stack with the largest at the bottom. Place a 12.7cm (5in) circular cake card on top, round off the top with a large cake knife. Round off the top of the bottom cake too and keep the offcuts.

4 Score round a 10cm (4in) circular cake card perched on the bottom tier as shown and carve out a hollow for the mouth.

5 Place some cake offcuts on top and carve to shape a dome for the head. Carve a slope down from the head with the large cake knife.

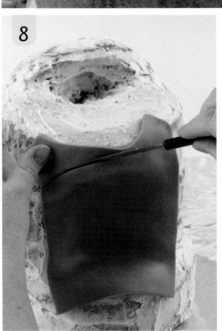

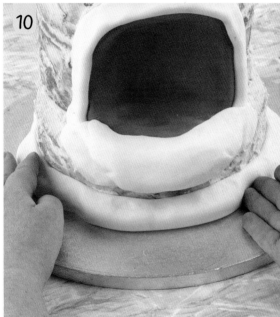

6   Cut out a central eye socket with a small knife.

7   Score and then cut wavy lines all the way round. Angle the small knife to cut out the top and then angle downwards to cut out the bottom.

8   Buttercream the whole cake. For the mouth, mix white, pink, grape violet and tangerine edible paste colours, mix into fondant (sugarpaste) and roll it out 2mm ($^1/_{16}$in) thick. Cut out a piece 16.5 x 11.5 (6½ x 4½in), push it into the mouth hole and trim.

9   Make a long sausage from 130g (4½oz) of white fondant (sugarpaste) and press it round the mouth to create the top lip. Smooth in the outer edges with your fingers.

10   Make a fat sausage from 250g (8¾oz) of white fondant (sugarpaste), flatten one side and push it onto the cake to make the bottom lip. Push it in randomly to make it wavy. Form 250g (8¾oz) of white fondant (sugarpaste) into a sausage long enough to go all around the base, push it onto the cake and press it to make it wobbly.

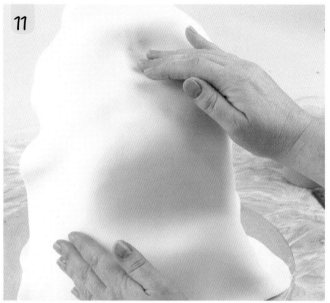

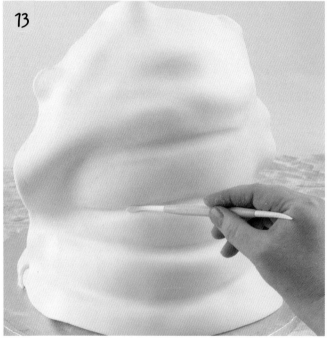

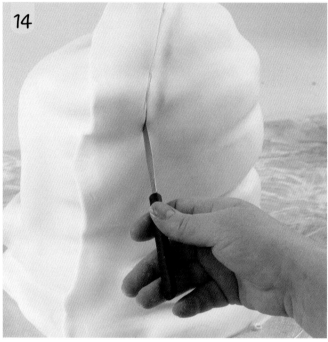

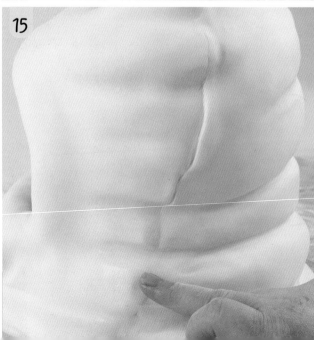

11 Knead 1.5kg of white fondant (sugarpaste). Roll out three-quarters of it 5mm ($^1/_8$in) thick to cover the front. Wet all the white fondant (sugarpaste) areas already on the cake. Drape the rolled-out piece over the front of the cake and push and smooth it into all the contours. Push the paste in the eye socket with a rolling pin. Don't worry if it tears.

12 Trim round the mouth and smooth in the edges. Trim the edges of the front piece.

13 Roll out the rest of the fondant (sugarpaste) and cover the back in the same way, overlapping the front piece. Smooth into all the grooves with your hands, then with a Dresden tool. Use the same tool to push under the paste at the base, then trim round.

14 Feel through the overlap for the join and trim just beyond it to avoid making a gap. Smooth in the join with a bit of water.

15 Smooth the joins, making sure the creases are continuous.

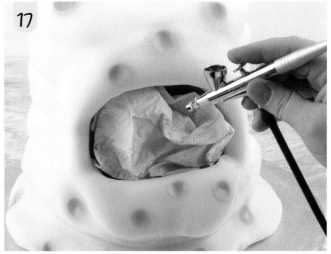

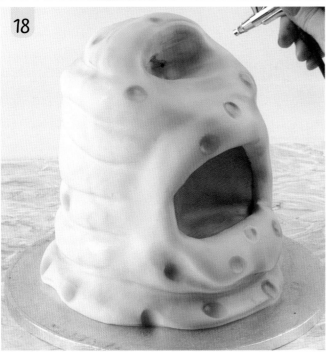

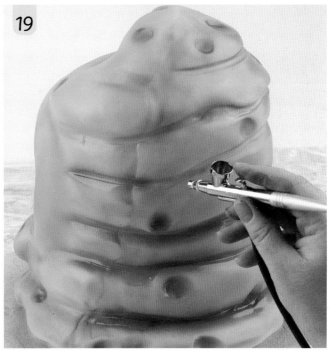

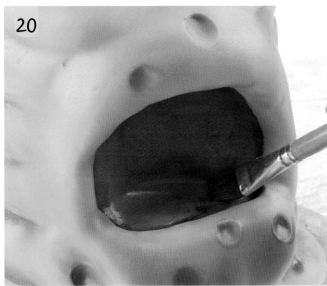

16 Create the welts by wetting a finger and placing on the monster's skin. Do not push, just allow the water to dissolve a dip in the surface. Be careful of drips which will also dissolve the fondant (sugarpaste). Allow to dry before airbrushing. Fill the airbrush with green and begin spraying the welts.

17 Fill with teal and a little alcohol to thin it. Put kitchen paper in the mouth to mask it and airbrush round it.

18 Continue airbrushing all over with teal.

19 Use a darker teal, with no alcohol, to airbrush the creases. Do not spray too much or it will pool on the surface. You can add another overall coat of darker teal if you need to.

20 Remove any teal colour from the mouth with a wet paintbrush.

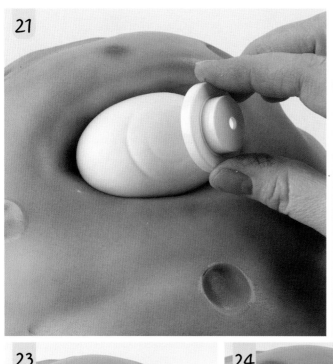

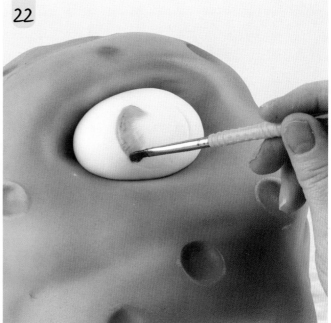

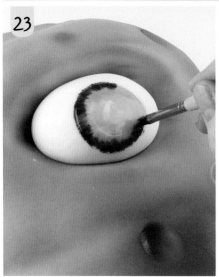

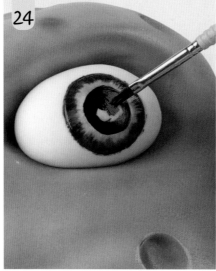

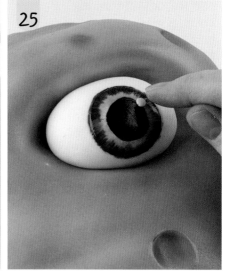

21 Make the eye from 100g (3½oz) of white modelling paste formed into an oval and place it in the socket. Imprint it with the circle in the centre of a garrett frill cutter.

22 Put some party green, holly and black edible paste colour in a clean paint palette with a little alcohol. Paint the green iris of the monster's eye with party green.

23 Paint a darker outline for the iris with holly and black.

24 Paint a large black pupil.

25 Highlight the pupil with a tiny circle of white fondant (sugarpaste).

26

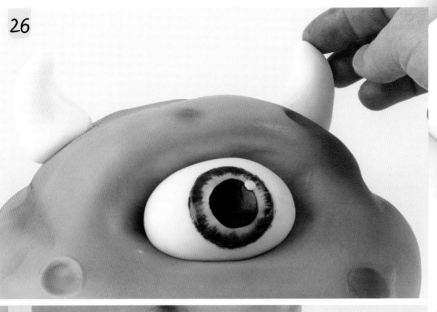

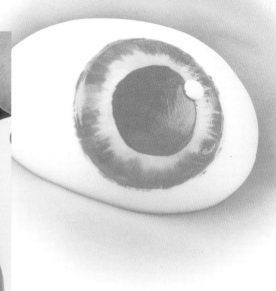

27

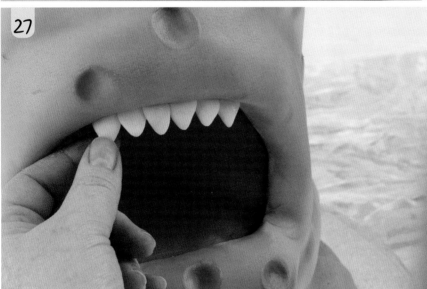

26 Make the horns from 60g (2oz) of white modelling paste shaped into a cone then curved. Find the best place on the head and stick them on with water.

27 Take 20g (¾oz) of white modelling paste and model pointed cones for the top teeth. The bottom teeth should be rectangular, with just two pointed fangs. Add water to the top teeth while still soft and attach.

28 Mix airbrush colour teal with 20g (¾oz) of white modelling paste and roll out to a small tapered sausage, then flatten and stick on for the eyelid. Trim if needed.

28

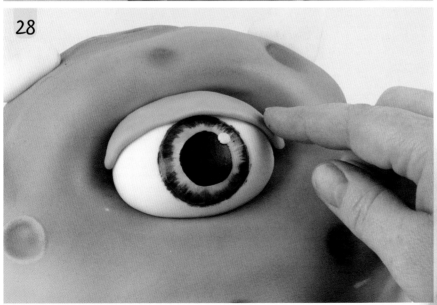

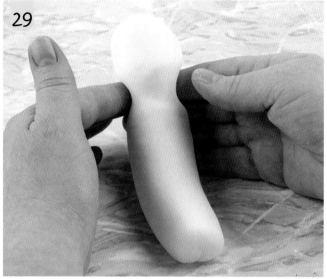

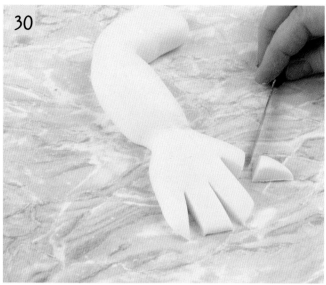

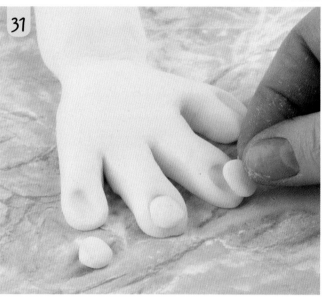

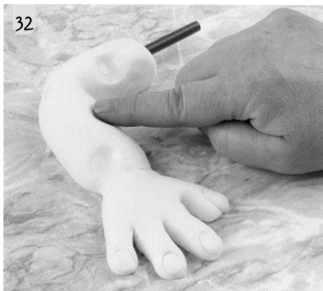

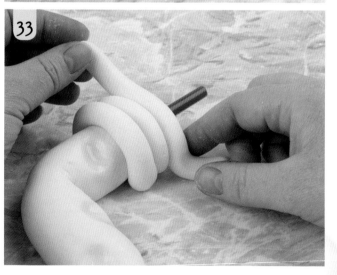

29 Make each arm from 275g (9¾oz) of fondant (sugarpaste) mixed with Tylose (CMC). Roll into a sausage, then roll between your fingers to create a wrist and elbow.

30 Flatten the hand and make three straight cuts to create fingers and a thumb. Spread out the fingers and thumb and trim the thumb to half its length.

31 Shape the fingers and press in fingernails using the wider end of the Dresden tool. Shape little fingernails and put them in.

32 Push a red poly dowel into the end and press with a wet finger to create welts.

33 Make sausages to create the coil effect for the shoulder join. Attach the arm to the monster, protect the surroundings with kitchen paper and airbush with teal airbrush colour.

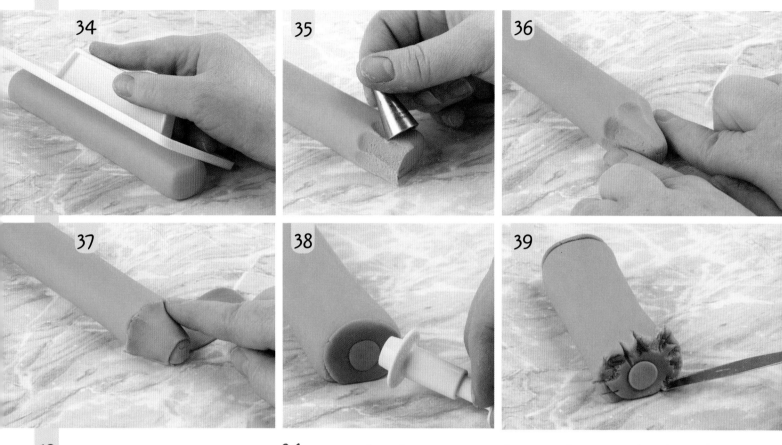

34 Roll 125g (4½oz) of orange fondant (sugarpaste) with Tylose (CMC) into a 15.2cm (6in) sausage and trim one end to straighten it. Use a smoother to flatten the sides to create the pencil shape.

35 Use a piping nozzle to scoop out paste, making the pencil look as though it has been sharpened with a knife.

36 Shape the end into a point with your fingers.

37 Cut a small strip of teddy bear brown fondant (sugarpaste) and smooth it in to look like the pencil wood, leaving the orange tip showing.

38 At the other end, roll a small ball of teddy bear brown and flatten it to make the wooden pencil end. Use a medium circle plunger cutter to cut and place a circle of the orange paste for the pencil core. Make several pencils in this way in different colours, and make some half pencils, as Messy Monster is meant to be causing havoc!

39 Make a chewed-looking half pencil by roughing up the end with a palette knife as shown.

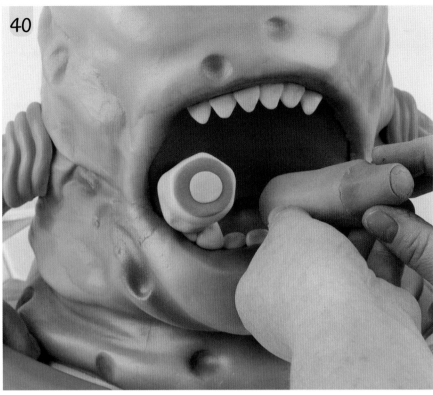

40 Insert a dampened piece of narrow poly dowel into the monster's mouth and push on a half pencil, then insert another poly dowel and another half pencil with the sharpened end pointing outwards.

41 For the paintbrush, roll 125g (4½oz) of dark brown fondant (sugarpaste) with Tylose (CMC) to a tapered sausage 12.7cm (5in) long. Cut across the ends and soften them with your fingers. For the brush, model a thick cone from 20g (¾oz) of mixed white and brown fondant (sugarpaste) with Tylose (CMC), one end flush with the handle and the other end tapering to a point. Texture it with the Dresden tool. To create the texture of the bristle ends, poke and flick with the Dresden tool. Make a strip of white fondant (sugarpaste) with Tylose (CMC) 3.8 x 6.4cm (1½ x 2½in), stick it on around the join and allow to dry. This will later be painted with satin silver edible lustre dust with alcohol.

42 Make a paint tube with 300g (10½oz) of white fondant (sugarpaste) with Tylose (CMC). Roll into a sausage, then flatten one end and cut straight across it, then emboss the flattened end with the Dresden tool to suggest the seal of the tube.

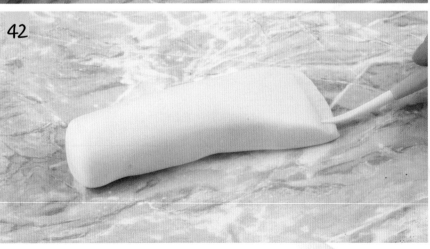

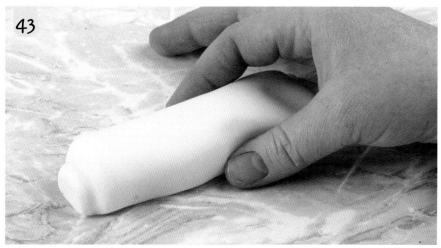

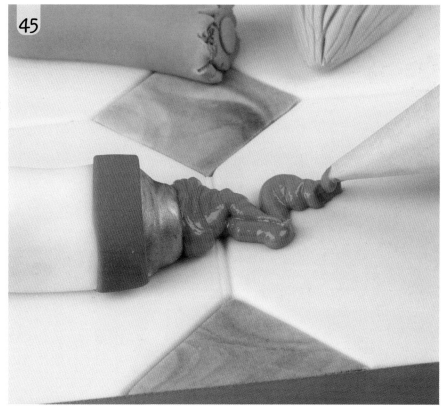

43 At the other end, model a cone shape and the neck of the tube, then cut across the neck to suggest a tube with the lid off. Pinch the tube to give it a used look.

44 Make two strips from red fondant (sugarpaste) with Tylose (CMC) and stick these to the tube. Paint the open end of the tube with a satin silver edible lustre dust with alcohol and a paintbrush. Make a second tube of paint in the same way – I have made mine purple.

45 Arrange the paint tubes, paintbrush and pencils on the cake drum. Make 150g (5¼oz) royal icing, colour it red and violet with edible paste colours and use a piping bag to pipe paint splodges coming from the tubes, on the floor, on the paintbrush and in the monster's mouth to complete the mayhem. Trim the edge of the cake drum with silver ribbon, attached using double-sided tape.

TEENAGE KICKS

This cake was designed with teenage girls in mind – hence the make-up decorations, but it could easily be adapted for a boy, or for different styles of shoe. Take your time with the carving and do a little at a time until you are happy with it.

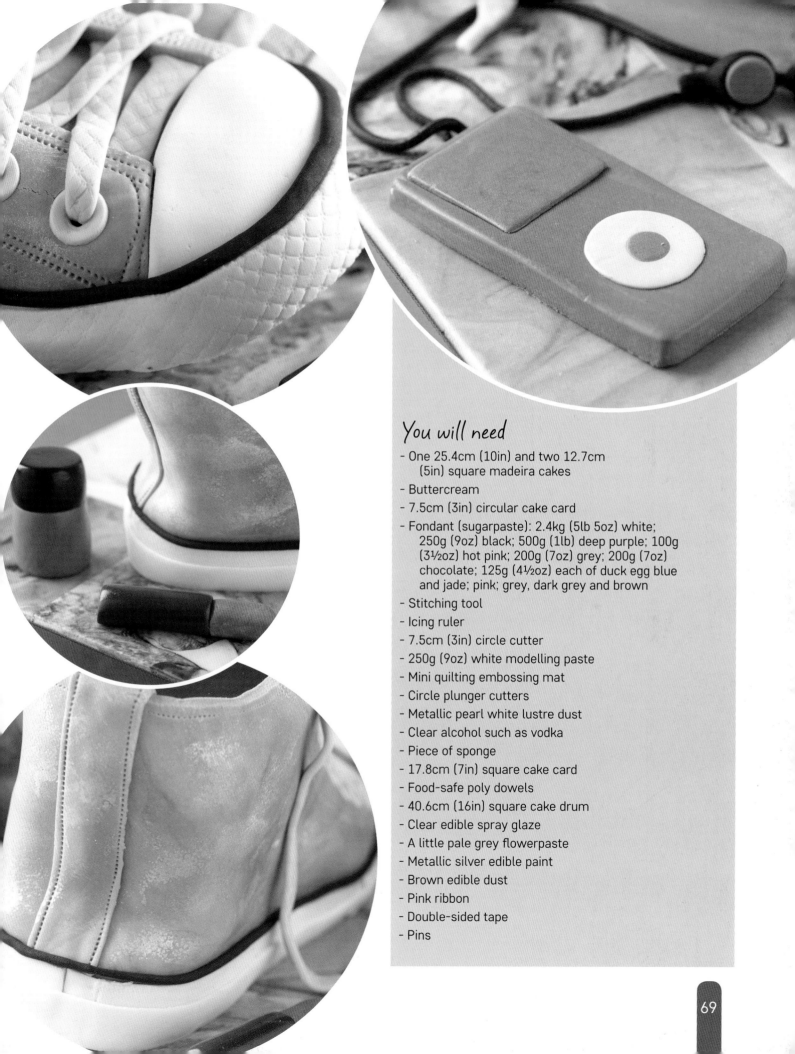

You will need

- One 25.4cm (10in) and two 12.7cm (5in) square madeira cakes
- Buttercream
- 7.5cm (3in) circular cake card
- Fondant (sugarpaste): 2.4kg (5lb 5oz) white; 250g (9oz) black; 500g (1lb) deep purple; 100g (3½oz) hot pink; 200g (7oz) grey; 200g (7oz) chocolate; 125g (4½oz) each of duck egg blue and jade; pink; grey, dark grey and brown
- Stitching tool
- Icing ruler
- 7.5cm (3in) circle cutter
- 250g (9oz) white modelling paste
- Mini quilting embossing mat
- Circle plunger cutters
- Metallic pearl white lustre dust
- Clear alcohol such as vodka
- Piece of sponge
- 17.8cm (7in) square cake card
- Food-safe poly dowels
- 40.6cm (16in) square cake drum
- Clear edible spray glaze
- A little pale grey flowerpaste
- Metallic silver edible paint
- Brown edible dust
- Pink ribbon
- Double-sided tape
- Pins

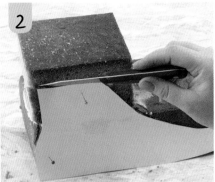

1 Level a 25.4cm (10in) square and two 12.7cm (5in) square cakes. Cut the large square in half and put a small square on top.

2 Stick one small square on top of the rectangle with buttercream and pin the shoe side template on page 138 onto the side. Count the pins for safety's sake. Score round the shape with a knife, then move the template to the other side of the cake, facing the same way of course, and repeat.

3 Carve round the template, checking both sides as you go.

4 Turn the cake over, pin on the sole template (page 139) and score and carve round it.

5 Place a 7.5cm (3in) circular cake card on top and sculpt round it.

6 Round off all the edges and create the shoe shape by shaving off little bits.

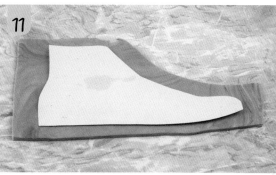

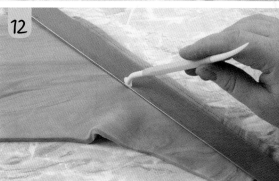

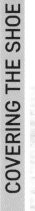

7 Cover with buttercream. Take 100g (3½oz) of black fondant (sugarpaste), roll out to 3mm (⅛in) thick, place it over the ankle part of the shoe and trim round it with a small knife.

8 For both shoes, take 1.25kg (2¾lb) of white fondant (sugarpaste) with 500g (1lb) of deep purple and marble them together (see page 22), then add 125g (4½oz) each of duck egg blue and jade and knead a little for a marbled effect. Take half for each shoe.

9 Cut into 150g (5¼oz) portions for parts of the shoe, to avoid overworking and spoiling the marbled effect. Roll a piece out to 21.5 x 7.5cm (8½ x 3in), trim the sides and bottom but keep the top rounded. Stitch round the curve with the stitching tool to make the tongue of the shoe.

10 Place on the shoe and smooth into the cake.

11 Take half of what is left and roll out 30.5 x 15.2cm (12 x 6in) for the side. Use the side template as a guide, but leave a wide margin.

12 Straighten the edge with the icing ruler as shown, ready for stitching. Stitch either side of the icing ruler, then move 3mm (⅛in) and repeat to create the stitching either side of the eyelets.

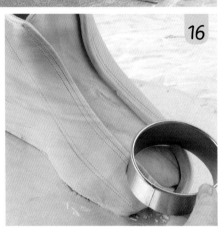

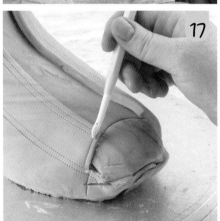

13 Brush the edge of the tongue and the black fondant (sugarpaste) with water and attach the side. Shape with your hands.

14 Hold a ruler against the back of the shoe and use a knife to emboss then trim the side. Run a Dresden tool round the bottom of the side to push it into the base, then trim. Turn the shoe side template over and repeat to make the other side.

15 Make a strip the width of the icing ruler and 16.5cm (6½in) long, stitch along either side and place it along the back seam of the shoe. Stitch round the top of the shoe. Curve the strip over the top.

16 Use a 7.5cm (3in) circle cutter to mark the toe cap curve.

17 Take out the excess fondant (sugarpaste) to allow for the toe cap and stitch round the edge.

18 Shape 30g (1oz) of rolled-out white fondant (sugarpaste) into a half circle, stick it on and trim it to shape. The underside of the sole needs to be white where it curves up, so roll out white modelling paste thinly, wet the underside of the toe cap, stick on the piece and trim.

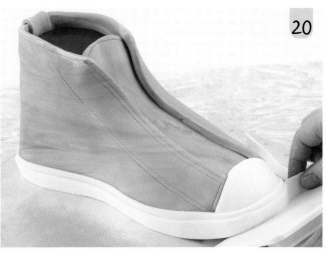

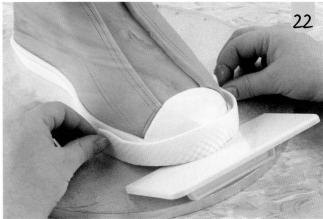

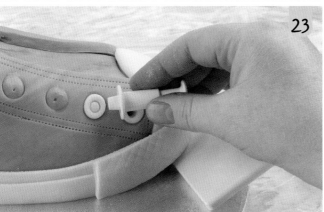

19 Make a strip of white modelling paste long enough to go all round the shoe and trim it to 2.5cm (1in) wide. Brush round the base of the shoe with water and attach the strip.

20 Make a 2cm (¾in) strip the same length and attach on top as shown. Place the tip of the shoe against a smoother as shown to hold it in place as it dries.

21 Make the textured front section of the trim. Cut a strip 21.5cm (8½in) long and 2.5cm (1in) wide and texture it with a mini quilting embossing mat. Line up the embossing mat carefully each time you move along the strip to keep the design consistent.

22 Place the textured strip evenly around the front of the shoe as shown and attach.

23 To make the eyelets, take the largest and smallest circle plunger cutters from the set. Use a ruler to mark 2.5cm (1in) intervals between the double stitching lines. Mark each hole with the large plunger cutter. Roll out white modelling paste very thinly, brush water on each eyelet and cut and place white circles using the large plunger cutter. Use the small plunger cutter to cut a circle in the centre.

24 Push in the centre of each eyelet with the handle end of a paintbrush.

25 Mix metallic pearl white edible lustre dust with alcohol, dip in a piece of sponge and randomly sponge a pattern on the shoe.

27 Take another section of the lace piece and pinch the ends. Dampen the insides of two eyelets with water and push each end of the lace secion inside, to create the diagonals. Continue lacing the shoe in this way.

26 To make the laces, mix white and purple fondant (sugarpaste), flatten with a smoother and cut to 5mm (¼in) wide. Texture with the mini quilting embossing mat as for the trim. Cut a short section and place it in the front of the shoe as shown, tucked under the sides.

28 Roll out black fondant (sugarpaste) very thinly, cut a 3mm (⅛in) strip and flatten with a smoother. Brush on water and stick on the trim as shown.

TIP

You may need to straighten the edges with a smoother every time you place a new tile.

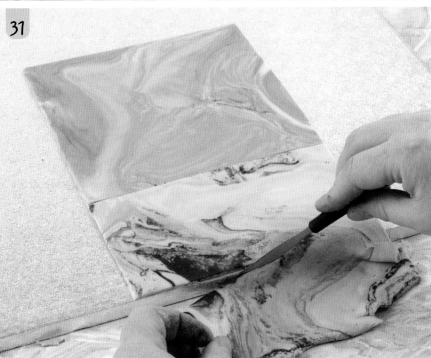

29 To create the tiled floor, take 1kg (2lb 2oz) of white fondant (sugarpaste) and divide it into three. Add between 10g ($^1/_3$oz) and 25g ($^4/_5$oz) of black fondant (sugarpaste) to each section and marble the black and white together to make one section light, one medium and one dark. Roll out using dowels for an even depth, then cut round a 17.8cm (7in) cake card to create the tile.

30 Place by eye in the centre of the 40.6cm (16in) cake drum, dampened with water, and straighten the sides with a smoother.

31 Make a contrasting tile, place it on the cake drum and trim. Continue to cover the whole cake drum. Leave to dry then spray with clear edible spray glaze.

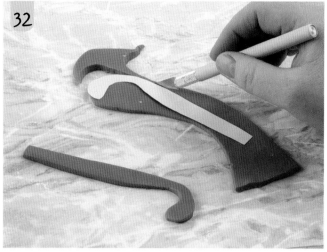

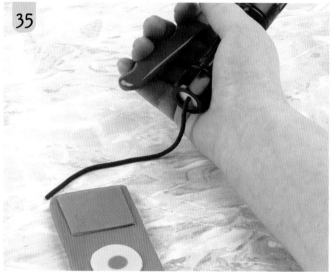

TIP

For all the detail modelling, use fondant (sugarpaste) strenghtnened with Tylose (CMC) unless stated otherwise.

32 Use the sunglasses template on page 139 to cut out an earpiece from pink paste, then flip and cut out the second.

33 Cut out the main sunglasses shape from black paste. Round the edges with your fingers. Cut out lenses from thinly rolled grey paste. Stick in place and smooth in with your fingers and a smoother. Place the sunglasses as if folded and spray with clear edible spray glaze.

34 To make the MP3 player, roll out pink paste 5mm ($^1/_8$in) deep and cut to 5 x 10cm (2 x 4in). Soften the edges. Roll out pale grey flowerpaste thinly and cut a circle using a large piping nozzle. Use a small plunger cutter to cut a circle from grey paste. Stick on the circles and flatten with a smoother.

35 Roll out dark grey paste, cut to 3.8cm (1½in) square, stick on as a screen and reshape with the edge of the smoother. Flatten with the smoother, allow the MP3 player to dry and spray with clear edible spray glaze. Make wires with black paste, using a clay gun (see page 23).

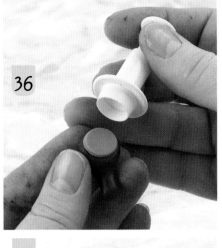

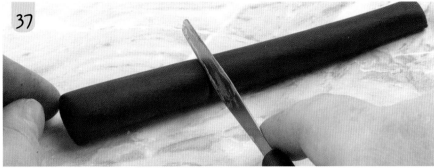

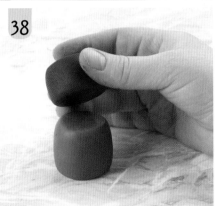

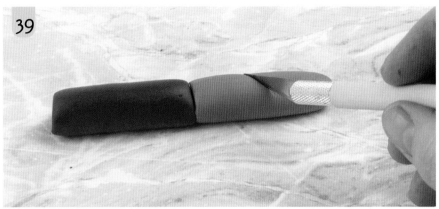

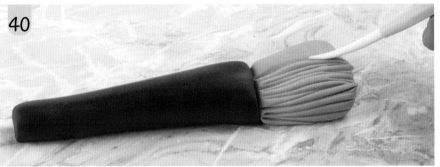

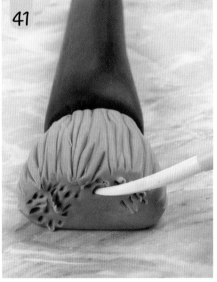

36 To make each earbud, roll black paste into a ball and roll with your fingers to make a neck. Flatten one side on the work surface. Roll out grey paste and cut and place a circle using a plunger cutter. Make a hole with any pointed tool to feed the wires into.

37 To make the mascara, roll a tapered sausage of black paste, 12.7cm (5in) long. Roll with a smoother and score with a knife 3.8cm (1½in) down to suggest the join of the lid. Spray with edible spray glaze.

38 To make the nail polish lid, roll a black ball and shape it into a squat cylinder 2.5cm (1in) in diameter. Roll purple paste into a ball and shape it into a deeper cylinder of the same diameter. Stick the lid to the pot. Spray with edible spray glaze.

39 For the lipstick, roll brown paste into a cylinder 5cm (2in) long. Roll a pink cylinder a fraction thinner, stick it to the brown part and cut across the pink at an angle as shown. Spray with edible spray glaze.

40 For the make-up brush, roll brown paste to a tapered sausage 12.7cm (5in) long. Cut across the ends and soften them with your fingers. For the brush, model a thick cone from 20g (¾oz) of mixed white and brown fondant (sugarpaste), one end flush with the handle and the other wider. Texture it with the Dresden tool.

41 To create the texture of the bristle ends, poke and flick with the Dresden tool. Make a strip of white paste 3.8 x 6.4cm (1½ x 2½in), stick it on around the join and allow to dry. Spray metallic silver edible paint into its lid and use a paintbrush to paint the white strip. To suggest make-up in the brush, dust the end with brown edible dust, leaving the base clean. Arrange all the pieces on the cake board and trim the edge with pink ribbon, attaching it using double-sided tape.

CATCH OF THE DAY

This is a personal favourite of mine as it is adapted from my Best in Show competition winner. This is the perfect cake for a true fisherman or fisherwoman. The wow factor comes from its hyper-realistic finish. You can adapt the basket shape or model a different fish if you prefer.

You will need

- Two 25.4 x 17.7cm (10 x 7in) rectangular madeira cakes
- Buttercream
- 45.7cm (18in) square cake drum
- 6kg (13lb 3½oz) white fondant (sugarpaste)
- 500g (1lb 2oz) black modelling paste
- Edible paste colours: chestnut, dark brown, caramel, burgundy, ivory, black and green
- Edible dust colours: plum, pink, pastel gold and white
- Icing ruler
- Clear alcohol such as vodka
- Clear edible spray glaze
- Metal mesh or silicone mould for fish scales
- Pearl, silver and black edible lustre sprays
- 750g (10½oz) royal icing
- 500g (1lb 2oz) modelling paste
- 5.7cm (2¼in) circle cutter
- Circle plunger cutters
- 250g (9oz) chocolate fondant (sugarpaste)
- Tylose (CMC)
- White vegetable fat
- Stitching wheel
- Small oval cutter
- Piping gel
- Brown ribbon and double-sided tape

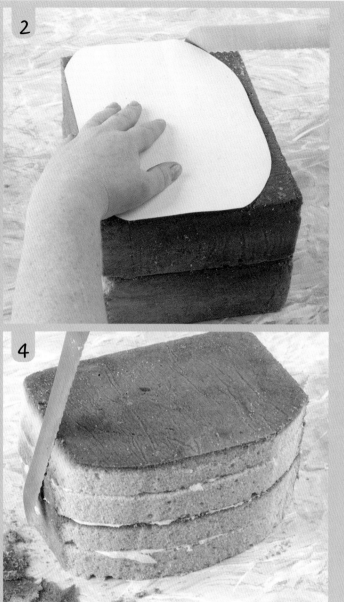

1 Take two rectangular cakes and level the tops. This can be done in the tins, or by measuring the height at the corners and scoring with a knife. Hold a ruler between the marks and slice off the top. Score the second cake by placing it next to the leveled first one.

3 Hold the knife vertically with the tip on the work surface and cut round the template shape.

2 Stack the cakes one on top of the other, with an uncut surface on top. Place the basket template (page 140) on top and score round it with the knife, then remove it.

4 You need to slice through the cake and add buttercream, so score level marks as before and slice through, then spread on buttercream. Angle the knife and cut round the top edges of the cake to taper it, creating the basket shape. Repeat at the bottom so that the basket tapers inwards.

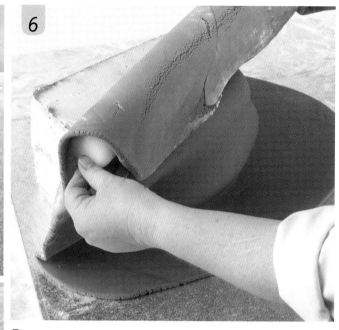

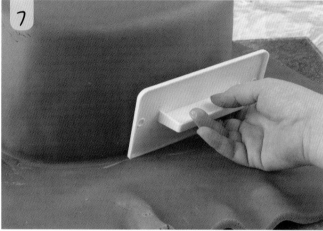

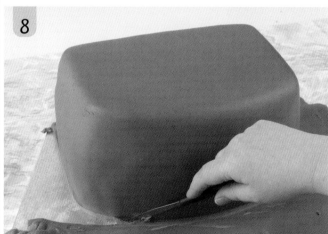

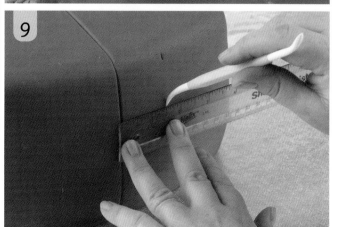

5   Stick the cake to the cake drum with a blob of buttercream, then use a palette knife to coat the whole cake with buttercream.

6   Colour 4kg (8lb 13oz) of fondant (sugarpaste) as shown on page 20, using chestnut and dark brown edible paste colours. Smear some of each colour on the fondant (sugarpaste) and knead the colours through, adding more as necessary, to achieve a chocolate brown. Roll out the fondant (sugarpaste) to 5mm (¼in) depth, lift it on the rolling pin and drape it over the cake. Smooth the covering over the cake with your hands.

7   Smooth round the whole cake with a smoother, then use the base of this to score a line round the bottom of the cake.

8   Trim off the excess with a palette knife.

9   Mark the cake ready for the basketweave. Begin by finding the centre using a ruler, then score a line down the centre of the top and front using a Dresden tool. Score marks 3.8cm (1½in) across from the centre at intervals, then join them to score a line parallel to the central line. Continue all across the basket.

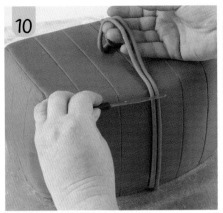

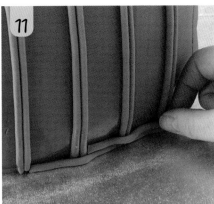

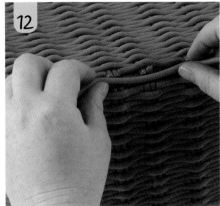

10 Make strands for the basketweave using the clay gun and fondant (sugarpaste) the same colour as the cake covering. Brush the cake with water, line up two strands on one of the scored lines and trim them to leave a gap at the top edge of the basket.

11 When all the uprights are done, cut horizontal pieces 9cm (3½in) long. Brush water along the bottom of the cake and place a strand as shown. Brush it into place to smooth it. Continue round the bottom of the basket. Brush water on again and place the next strands as shown, alternating with the first strands. Continue to cover the whole basket and lid.

12 Wet the top edge and place a horizontal strand all around the basket.

13 Make pieces 2cm (¾in) long and place these over the horizontal stand as shown, to trim the top edge. Allow the basket to dry.

14 Mix dark brown and chestnut edible paste colour with alcohol and paint the whole basket. Allow to dry, then spray on clear edible spray glaze.

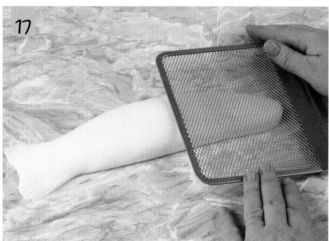

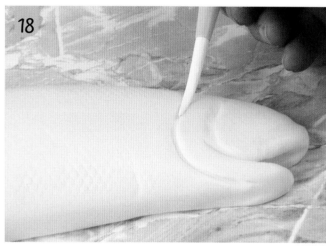

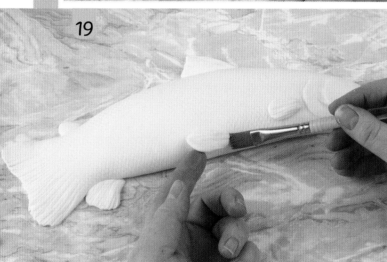

15 Roll 500g (1lb 2oz) of fondant (sugarpaste) into a long, tapered sausage, and flatten it to form the fish.

16 Shape the dip in the tail with a knife. Texture the tail with the Dresden tool as shown.

17 Emboss the scale pattern into the fish using a silicone mould or a piece of metal mesh.

18 Shape the front end of the fish and cut the mouth with a knife. Mould the inside of the mouth with the Dresden tool. Sculpt the detail of the face and gills as shown using the wider end of the Dresden tool.

19 Make five tapered sausages from 50g (2oz) of fondant (sugarpaste) and flatten them into fin shapes. Three should be more triangular, and one should be larger than the others. Texture them with the Dresden tool as for the tail. Brush the fish with a little water in the places shown in the picture, and place the fins.

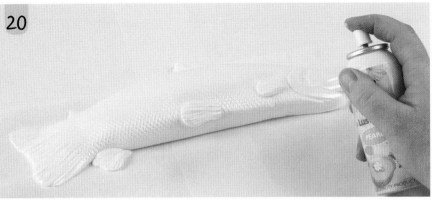

20 Protect your work surface for spray painting. Spray the bottom of the fish with pearl edible lustre spray.

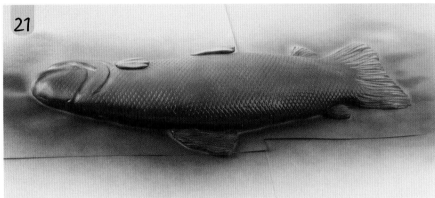

21 Spray the rest of the fish with silver edible lustre spray, then turn it round and spray a line of black along the top.

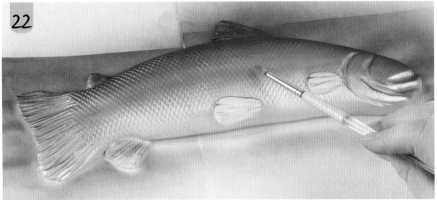

22 Brush pink edible dust colour into the fish's mouth and along the middle of the fish.

23 Take a tiny bit of fondant (sugarpaste), roll it into a ball and flatten it to make the eye, then push this into the face. Mix pastel gold lustre dust and alcohol, and paint the eye. Mix black edible paste colour with alcohol and paint the pupil of the eye and a ring around it.

24 Use the same mix to dab dots all over the fish as shown.

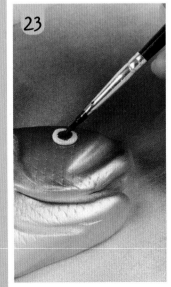

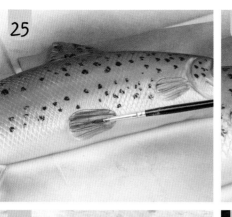

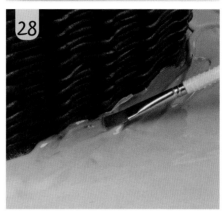

25 Mix brown edible paste with alcohol and paint the fins as shown.

26 Paint around the mouth with the brown paint mix. Allow to dry, then spray with clear edible spray glaze.

27 Marble together 1kg (2¼lb) of black and white fondant (sugarpaste) and roll the results in your hands to make grey pebbles of varying shapes, sizes and tone (see page 78). Do the same with white fondant (sugarpaste) marbled with some that has been coloured with caramel and ivory edible paste colours to make brown pebbles.

28 Colour 750g (10½oz) of royal icing with ivory, chestnut, caramel and dark brown edible paste colour to create the sand. Spread this on the cake drum around the basket with a large palette knife. Use a damp brush to push it into the edges of the basket.

29 Place the pebbles all over the 'sand'.

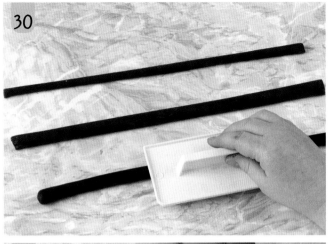

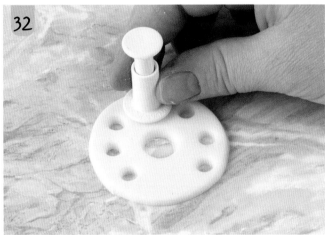

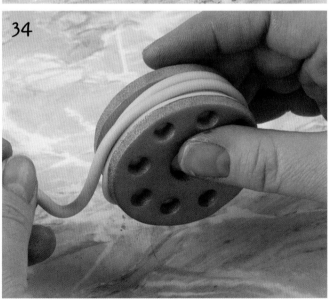

30 Roll out a very long sausage from 500g (1lb 2oz) of black modelling paste. Use a smoother to roll it into a rod shape, thinner at one end than at the other. This will be a section of the fishing rod. Cut it into three pieces of ascending size, and smooth again.

31 Roll out a little black fondant (sugarpaste) and cut a straight strip, then stick this to the smallest rod section with water, to make the screw-in part of the fishing rod. Add another one to the next size up.

32 Roll out 100g (3½oz) of modelling paste 3mm (⅛in) thick and cut two circles of 5.7cm (2¼in) circumference. Cut out the centres with the largest of a set of circle plunger cutters, then cut out smaller circles around the edge. Cut out holes directly opposite each other first, as on a clock face, then divide up the gaps, to ensure even spacing. Spray both sides with silver edible lustre spray and leave to dry.

33 Colour 30g (1oz) of fondant (sugarpaste) green and make a thick disk 4.4cm (1¼in) across. Use water to stick this to one of the silver circles and stick the other one on top to make the reel.

34 Make a very long sausage from green-coloured fondant (sugarpaste), either using a clay gun or just rolling and then tidying with a smoother. Wind this round the reel as the fishing line.

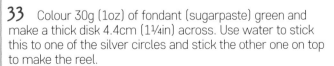

35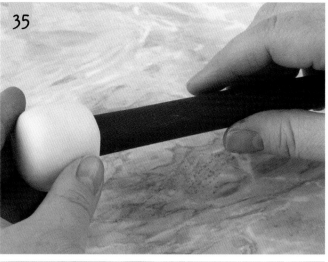

36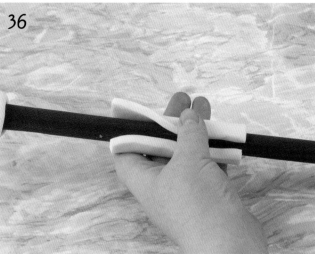

37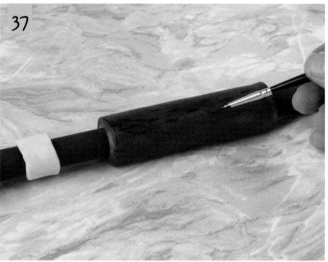

38

35 Make a handle for the widest rod section from a 250g (9oz) ball of white fondant (sugarpaste), and push this onto the rod end.

36 Roll out white fondant (sugarpaste) to 5mm (¼in) depth, cut a rectangle 9cm (3½in) long and wide enough to go round the widest rod section. Wrap it round as shown, to make the cork grip.

37 Make a smaller strip and add this beside the first, as shown. Paint the cork grip with mixed brown and chestnut edible paste colour, then use a finer brush to add flecks of a darker brown, to look like cork. Paint the rod end made in step 35 in the same way.

38 Spray silver edible lustre spray into the lid and use a brush to paint this onto the narrower strip.

39 Make a tiny eyelet shape from a sausage of modelling paste curled round and attach it to the rod with water. When dry, paint it in the same way to look like metal.

39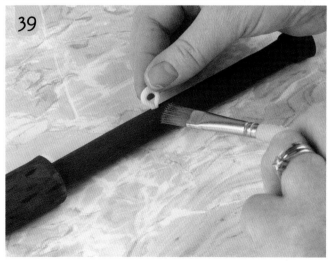

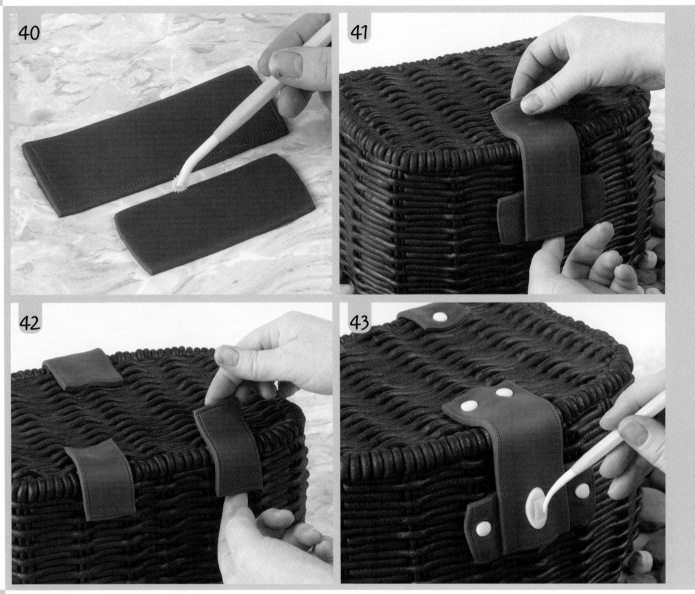

40 Roll out 250g (9oz) chocolate fondant (sugarpaste) 3mm (¹/₈in) thick and cut two straps, one 5 x 10cm (2 x 4in) and one 5 x 14cm (2 x 5½in). Use the stitching wheel to decorate the edges.

41 Use water to stick the smaller piece on horizontally on the front of the basket, and the larger one verically as shown.

42 Cut out, stitch and place two more of the smaller strips to make hinges at the back.

43 To make the studs for the straps, make little indentations with a ball tool, roll little balls of fondant (sugarpaste), flatten them and place them in the indentations where shown.

44 Roll out fondant (sugarpaste) to 5mm (¼in) depth. Use a small oval cutter to cut out a clasp and stick this on with water where shown. Use the Dresden tool to emboss it with a rectangle. Make a very small sausage shape and emboss two lines in it, then stick it to the clasp as shown. When dry, paint the studs and clasp silver by spraying silver lustre spray into the lid, then brushing it on.

45 Apply piping gel to the pebbles to make them look wet, then place the rod parts and finally the fish. As a finishing touch, trim the edge of the cake drum with brown ribbon, attached using double-sided tape.

ANYONE FOR TENNIS?

This cake is for tennis lovers and players. It is easy to carve and can easily be personalised for your favourite grass court champion.

You will need

- One 30.5cm (12in) square madeira cake
- Buttercream
- Ruler
- 3kg (6lb 10oz) white fondant (sugarpaste) for cake, cake drum and racket handle
- 43cm (17in) square cake drum
- 3.8cm (1½in) masking tape
- Scouring pad
- Blue, black and green airbrush colours
- 650g (1lb 7oz) black fondant (sugarpaste)
- 170g (6oz) black modelling paste
- Tylose (CMC)
- Edible paste colours: melon and party green
- Narrow food-safe poly dowels
- Zip impression mould
- Kitchen paper
- Cupcake pod
- 300g (10½oz) white modelling paste
- Small amount of royal icing (see page 13)
- Clear edible spray glaze
- Green ribbon and double-sided tape

1 Cut the cake in half and stack one half on top of the other. Buttercream together. Measure and mark 11.5cm (4½in) across the top and cut off the edge to narrow the cake.

2 Cut across the cake near the centre and place the off-cut in the gap as shown to make a cake that is 34.5cm (13½in) long. Buttercream all the pieces together.

3 Make a card template from the one on page 141 and hold it against one side. Score round it with a sharp knife. Do the same on the other side with the template facing in the same direction.

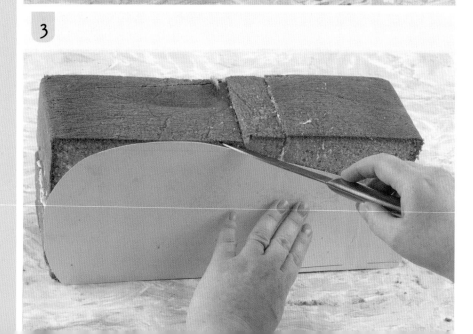

4 Sculpt round the bag shape as shown. Round off the edges slightly and take a litle bit off the bottom at each side.

5 Buttercream the cake and cover it with 1.5kg (3lb 5oz) of white fondant (sugarpaste). Trim the edges with a small palette knife and tuck them under with the Dresden tool. Leave to firm off, ideally overnight.

6 Coat a 43cm (17in) square cake drum with white fondant (sugarpaste). Place a strip of 3.8cm (1½in) masking tape 5cm (2in) from one side. Stipple the icing with a clean, dry scouring pad to create the texture of a grass tennis court

7 Put green airbrush colour in the airbrush bowl and try out on scrap paper, then spray the covered cake drum green. Apply several coats, leaving twenty minutes' drying time between each one. Finish with a darker mix made from three-quarters of a bowl of green with one drop of black.

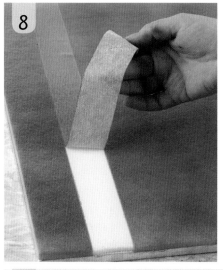

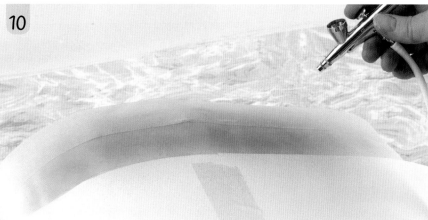

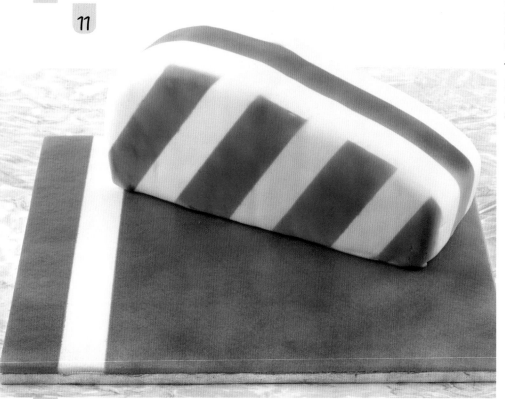

8 Remove the masking tape to reveal the white tennis court line.

9 Create the diagonal stripes on the tennis bag using the same masking tape, making sure they are evenly spaced. Do one side first, masking off the top of the bag. Fill the airbrush with blue colour and use it on its lowest speed. If the masking tape lifts away from the icing, hold it down with a paintbrush.

10 Remove the masking tape from the top of the bag and place two strips to create a blue stripe along the middle, protecting the side you have already done with paper. Repeat step 9 to complete the other side of the bag.

11 Remove the masking tape and leave the bag to dry, then place it carefully on the covered cake drum as shown.

12   Take 50g (1¾oz) of black fondant (sugarpaste) and roll out a long sausage. When it is around 7mm (¼in) wide, roll it with a smoother to 56cm (22in) long.

13   Apply water with the waterbrush, being careful not to wet the blue too much, and apply the black trim as shown.

14   Apply more of the black trim across the bottom and cut to make a neat join.

15   Make the zip as for the beading and cut it to 53.5cm (21in) long. Use a zip impression mould to create the texture.

16   Push the zip with two smoothers to neaten the edges.

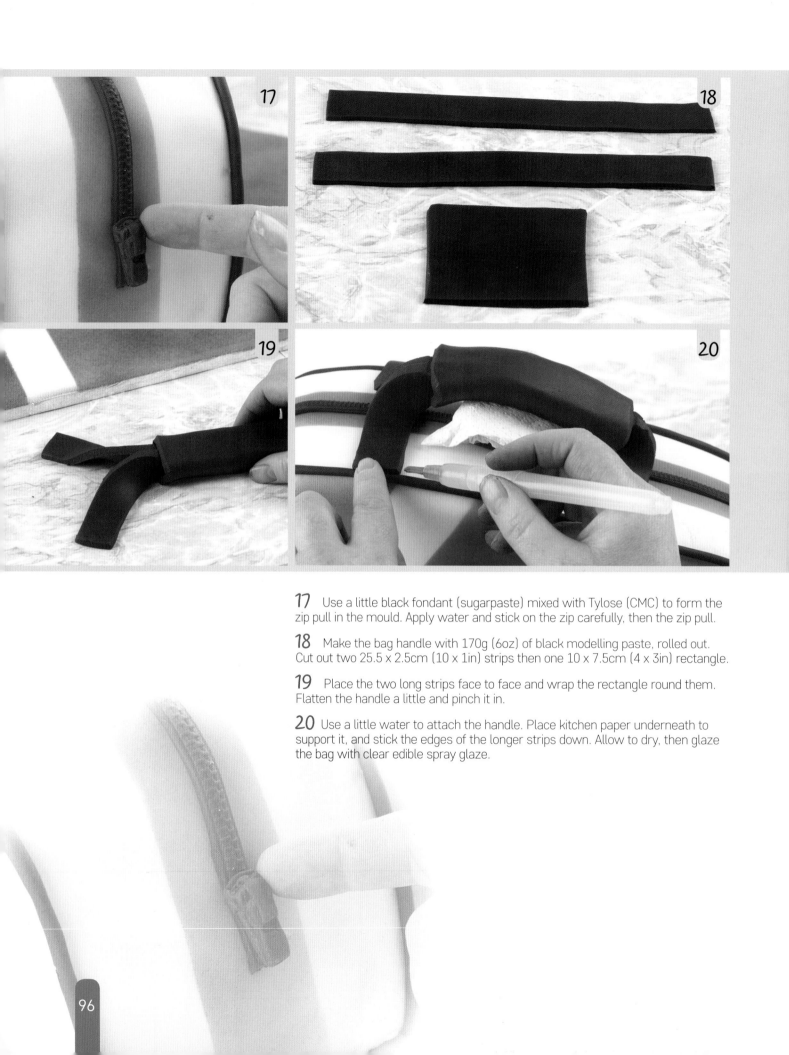

17 Use a little black fondant (sugarpaste) mixed with Tylose (CMC) to form the zip pull in the mould. Apply water and stick on the zip carefully, then the zip pull.

18 Make the bag handle with 170g (6oz) of black modelling paste, rolled out. Cut out two 25.5 x 2.5cm (10 x 1in) strips then one 10 x 7.5cm (4 x 3in) rectangle.

19 Place the two long strips face to face and wrap the rectangle round them. Flatten the handle a little and pinch it in.

20 Use a little water to attach the handle. Place kitchen paper underneath to support it, and stick the edges of the longer strips down. Allow to dry, then glaze the bag with clear edible spray glaze.

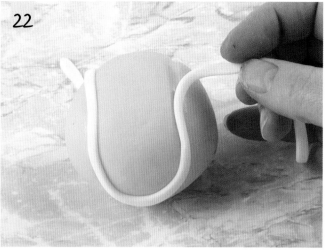

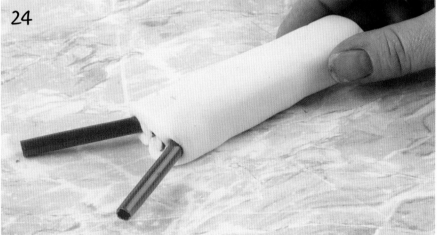

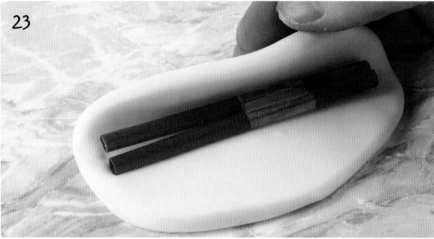

21 Mix melon and party green edible paste colours into white modelling paste, take 115g (4oz), roll it into a ball and stipple it with the scouring pad to create texture. Indent the S-shaped seam with a Dresden tool.

22 Take 10g (¼oz) of white modelling paste and roll with the smoother into a very thin sausage, then flatten. Wet the seam area on the ball, place the sausage and smooth with the smoother. Leave the ball to dry in the rounded lid of a cupcake pod.

23 Cut two pieces of narrow poly dowel into 10cm (4in) strips. Tape them together and with a little water, wrap white modelling paste around them to make the tennis racket handle.

24 Cut two 5cm (2in) pieces of the same poly dowel to make the V part of the racket frame that attaches to the handle. With a little water, stick them into the handle as shown.

25 Wrap the V part in modelling paste as before.

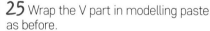

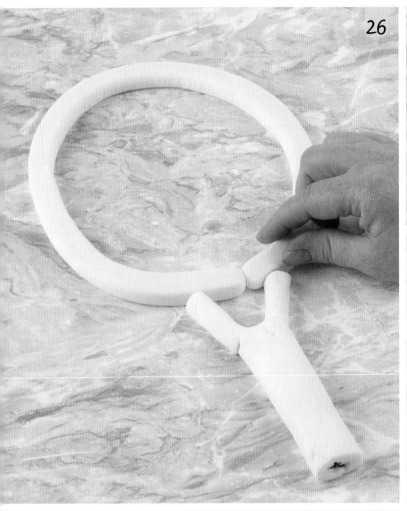

26 Take 160g (5½oz) of white modelling paste for the racket head and roll it out to 56cm (22in) long and 13mm (½in) thick. Flatten the top and sides with the smoother. Shape into the racket head.

27 Roll out 250g (8¾oz) of black fondant (sugarpaste), lift it over the racket with a rolling pin and stretch it to cover the racket as shown. Score round the edges, trim neatly and tuck under with a Dresden tool.

28 Take 50g (2oz) white fondant (sugarpaste), roll out to 10 x 5cm (4 x 2in), cover the handle and trim the edges.

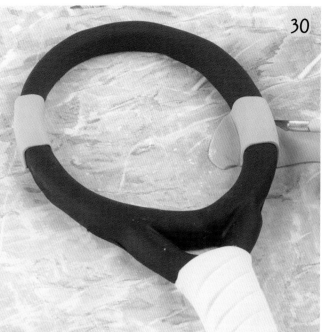

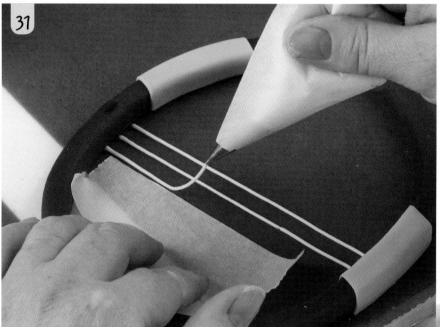

29 Score diagonal lines across the handle with the Dresden tool. Allow it to dry, then glaze it with clear edible spray glaze.

30 Take 30g (1oz) of white modelling paste, colour it with the same airbrush colour as the bag, roll it out and cut strips for the frame. Stick these to the frame as shown and trim neatly.

31 Fill a piping bag with white royal icing, and fit a no. 2 nozzle. Use masking tape as a guide to help you pipe the lines for the racket strings. Allow the strings going in one direction to dry for two hours, then pipe in the other direction, again using masking tape as a guide but not sticking it down. Arrange all the pieces on the cake board and trim the edge with green ribbon using double-sided tape.

WHAT'S BAKING?

This is the perfect cake for a keen baker! I really enjoyed making this one as it captures the messy reality of a busy cook's kitchen. You can adapt this design by changing the colour of the mixer and worktop, and of course you can change the baking ingredients too.

You will need

- 45.7cm (18in) square cake drum
- 2kg (4lb 6oz) white fondant (sugarpaste)
- 500g (1lb 2oz) grey fondant (sugarpaste)
- Black airbrush colour
- Pot of edible silver glitter flakes
- 23cm (9in) and 12.7cm (5in) square madeira cakes
- Two circular 12.7cm (5in) madeira cakes, 10cm (4in) deep
- Buttercream
- 10cm (4in) and 7.5cm (3in) circular cake cards
- 7.5cm (3in) and 23cm (9in) square cake cards
- 1kg (2lb 2oz) red fondant (sugarpaste)
- Eggs in an egg box
- Tylose (CMC)
- Clear edible spray glaze
- Edible silver and gold lustre spray
- 650g (1lb 7oz) cream fondant (sugarpaste)
- 700g (1lb 8½oz) royal icing
- A little icing (powdered) sugar
- 620g (1lb 6oz) marzipan
- Edible wafer paper
- Edible paste colours: cream, brown, chestnut, dark brown, melon and yellow
- Edible dust colours: silver, chocolate brown
- Clear alcohol such as vodka
- Chocolate chips
- 40g (1½oz) white flowerpaste
- White vegetable fat
- Clear piping gel
- Wide and narrow food-safe poly dowels
- Black edible pen
- Cocktail stick
- Black ribbon and double-sided tape

1 Cover the cake drum in 1.7kg (3lb 12oz) of white fondant (sugarpaste). Fill the airbrush with black and spray the whole cake drum, making sure you catch the edges of the icing too. Use several coats, with twenty minutes' drying time in between. Sprinkle on edible silver glitter flakes and allow to dry. Glaze with clear edible spray glaze.

2 Take the 23cm (9in) square cake and cut it into two equal rectangles. Place the smaller square cake on top of one rectangle as shown. Trim to fit and buttercream them together. Pin the mixer template (page 142) to the side and score round it with a sharp knife. Repeat on the other side, making sure the template faces in the same direction.

3 Cut off the top in line with the scored lines, then carve the shape with your cake knife. Keep an eye on the other side, as the knife goes right through.

4 Place a 10cm (4in) circular cake card on the base of the mixer shape as shown and carve round it to create the curve.

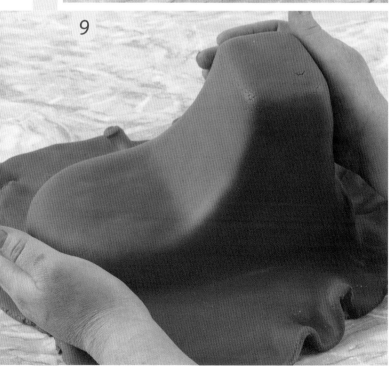

5 Place a square 7.5cm (3in) cake card on top, marking each side. Use this as a guide to carve down and outwards, creating the curved shape of the upright.

6 Soften all the edges a little by carving off hard lines with a sharp knife.

7 Take the remaining cake half and cut it to 5cm (2in) deep. Use the mixer arm template (page 142) to score and then carve the shape.

8 Round off the top edge as shown.

9 Buttercream both parts of the mixer and cover them with red fondant (sugarpaste). Roll out, drape over and shape with your hands and a smoother as usual. Indent the bottom edges with a smoother and trim neatly, tucking under with the Dresden tool. Glaze both parts with clear edible spray glaze.

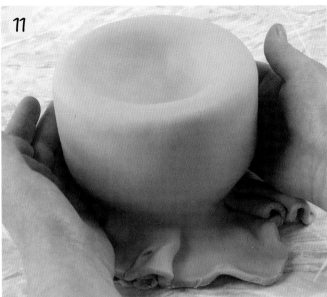

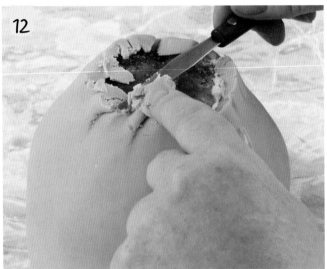

10 Take one of the circular madeira cakes to make the bowl of the mixer. Use a 7.5cm (3in) circular cake card to score the bottom of the bowl, and use the marks as a guide to carve the curved base as shown. Turn right side up. Score round a 10cm (4in) circular cake card to create the inner rim of the bowl. Remove the card, put the knife in at an angle so as not to cut too deeply, then continue carving freehand to hollow out the inside of the bowl.

11 Buttercream the bowl. Roll out 500g of grey fondant (sugarpaste) and use it to cover the bowl.

12 Turn the bowl over and trim the sugarpaste carefully at the bottom. This will help to flatten the top rim against the work surface.

13 Use a small rolling pin to define the rim. Don't worry too much how the grey paste looks inside the bowl, as it will be covered in royal icing.

14 Spray with edible silver lustre spray to give it a metallic look.

15 Take the other 12.7cm (5in) round cake and cut it in half horizontally to make two china bowls. Round off the bottom of each one as in step 10, but leave the tops flat. Place the bowls upside down and buttercream the sides and bottoms. Roll out 650g (1lb 7oz) of cream fondant (sugarpaste) and cover and trim each bowl.

16 Add Tylose (CMC) to the remaining cream fondant (sugarpaste) or use modelling paste. Make a long sausage and roll it to a strip 46 x 2.5cm (18 x 1in). Cut one long edge but shape the other one with a smoother so that it is more rounded. This will be the top of the bowl rim. Place a bowl the right way up, dampen the rim and stick it to the bowl, proud of the edge as shown. Trim neatly with a small palette knife. Wet the join with the waterbrush and smooth together with your fingers. Repeat for the second bowl.

17 Place 106ml (3½ fl oz) of white royal icing in one of the bowls, leaving the top rough as though it is cake mix. Sprinkle on icing (powdered) sugar to make it look floury.

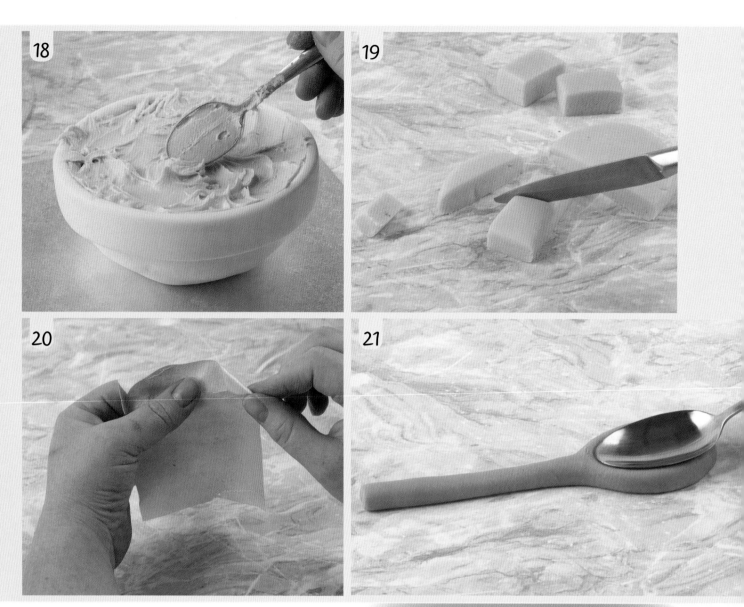

18 Mix cream and brown edible paste colours into 8 teaspoons of royal icing and place in the other bowl, leaving the top looking messy.

19 Roll out 500g (1lb 2oz) of marzipan 2.5cm (1in) thick, to make the butter. Cut it into little blocks. Glaze a little with clear edible spray glaze.

20 Take a piece of edible wafer paper for the butter wrapping. Spray it with edible gold lustre spray and allow to dry. Hold it over a steaming kettle so that it will bend, then bend and curl it a little ready to display.

21 Take 60g (2oz) marzipan for the wooden spoon and colour it with chestnut and a little melon edible paste colours. Roll into a sausage leaving one end wide, then press a spoon in the wide end to form the bowl of the wooden spoon. Make two spoons.

22   To make the cookies, take 200g (7oz) of fondant (sugarpaste) coloured with chestnut and dark brown edible paste colours and a touch of melon. For each cookie, shape 40g (1½oz) into a disk and poke at it with a bulbous cone tool for texture, then push it down a little. Press in chocolate chips.

23   Use a brush to apply chocolate edible dust.

24   To make the eggshells, roll out 40g (1½oz) white flowerpaste very thinly. Rub a little white vegetable fat onto a real egg and wrap the flowerpaste around it. Trim it in jagged lines to suggest the broken top of a shell.

25   To make the lower part of each eggshell, wrap a bit more flowerpaste round and egg and proceed as before. Leave all the eggshells to dry.

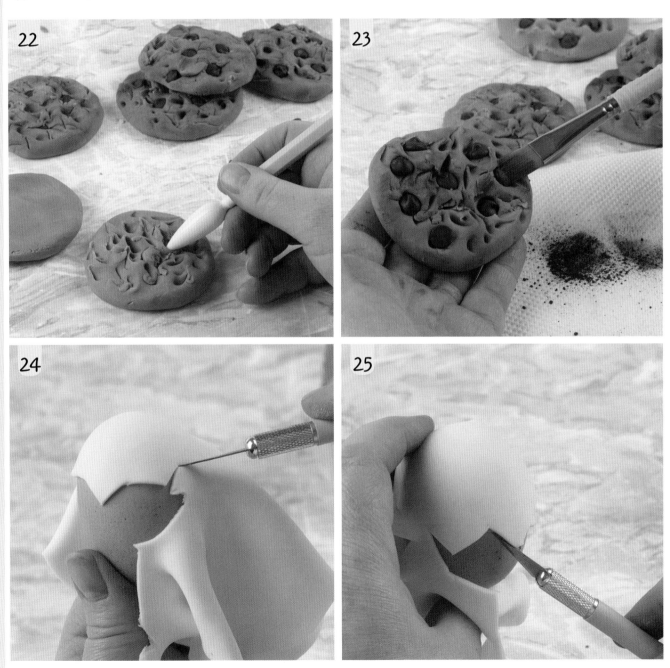

26 To make the egg yolks, take 60g (2oz) of white fondant (sugarpaste) coloured with yellow edible paste colour. Divide into three balls and flatten then. Brush clear piping gel onto the insides of the eggshells.

27 Place one of the yolks in an eggshell and spoon over clear piping gel.

28 Place two yolks in the floury bowl and spoon over four tablespoons of clear piping gel.

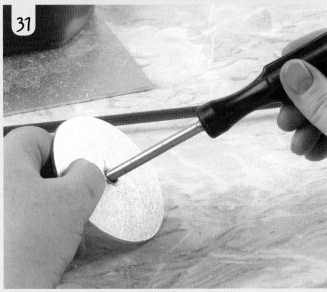

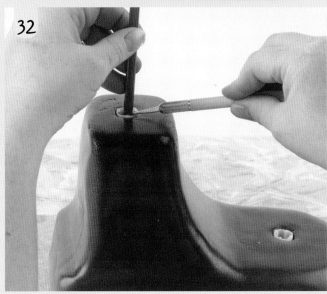

29 You now need to add some strength and structure to the base of the mixer. Take a length of wide white poly dowel and push it down into the tall part of the base as shown, right down to the board. Mark the height, take the poly dowel out and cut it to that height, then push it back in.

31 Mark the centre of a 7.5cm (3in) circular cake card and push in a sterilised screwdriver.

30 Do the same in the shorter part of the mixer base, where the bowl will go. Mark, cut and fit a length of wide poly dowel here.

32 Cut a length of narrow poly dowel to the same height as the tall part of the mixer.

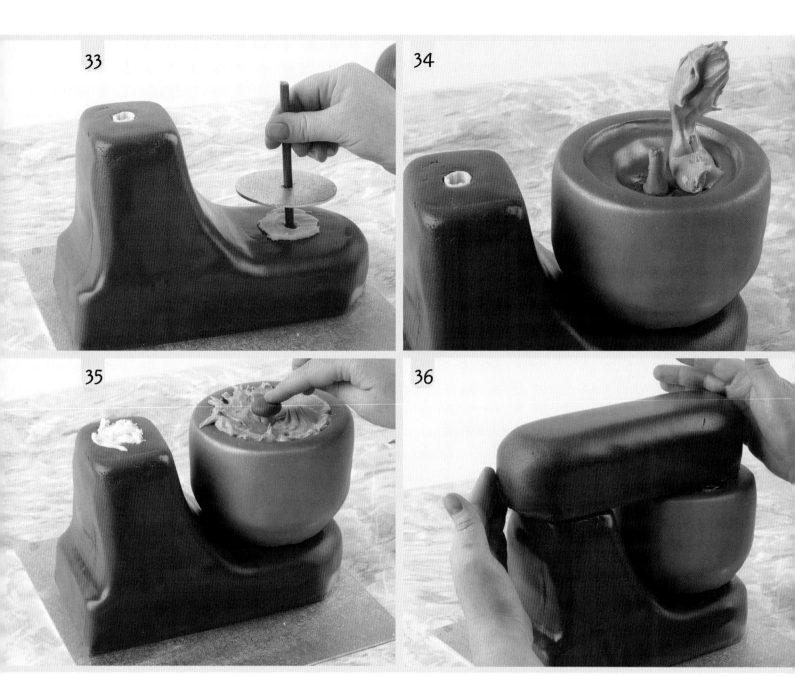

33 Fill the wide poly dowel in the shorter side of the mixer with royal icing, then spread some more royal icing on the base as shown. Push the length of narrow poly dowel cut in the previous step through the circular cake card, and place it inside the wider poly dowel. Push the cake card down. This will support the mixer bowl.

35 Place a little royal icing on top of the tall part of the mixer, and a ball of red fondant (sugarpaste) on top of the bowl as shown.

34 Carefully lower the mixer bowl onto the dowel. If the bowl is too high, you can trim it at the base and try again. Roll a little grey fondant (sugarpaste) over the red dowel end and spray it with edible silver lustre spray. Allow to dry. Place some royal icing, coloured as for the cake mix, into the bowl.

36 Place the arm of the mixer on top.

37 Roll a long sausage from 30g (1oz) of red fondant (sugarpaste). Dampen the join between the mixer base and the arm, and wrap the sausage around. Make a thinner sausage from grey fondant (sugarpaste) and wrap this round the base of the bowl. Paint it with edible silver lustre spray.

38 Roll out 50g (1¾oz) of grey fondant (sugarpaste) and cut a rectangle 10 x 2.5cm (4 x 1in). Score a groove and mark 'speeds' with black edible pen.

39 Stick the plaque on the mixer, dampening first with water, and use a smoother to straighten the sides. Make a knob from black fondant (sugarpaste) and attach it to the mixer with a length of cocktail stick and water. Arrange all the other items on the decorated cake drum and as a finishing touch, trim the edge with black ribbon, attached using double-sided tape.

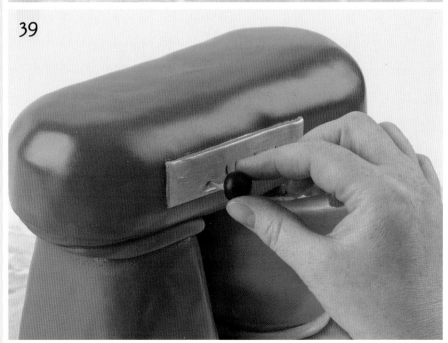

TOY TRAIN

This cake was designed for a small child's birthday, but it can also
be made for a christening instead of a traditional cake. You could
have open carriages filled with sweets or spell out the child's name
on the blocks. The wooden floor effect board can be used
as the base for a variety of projects.

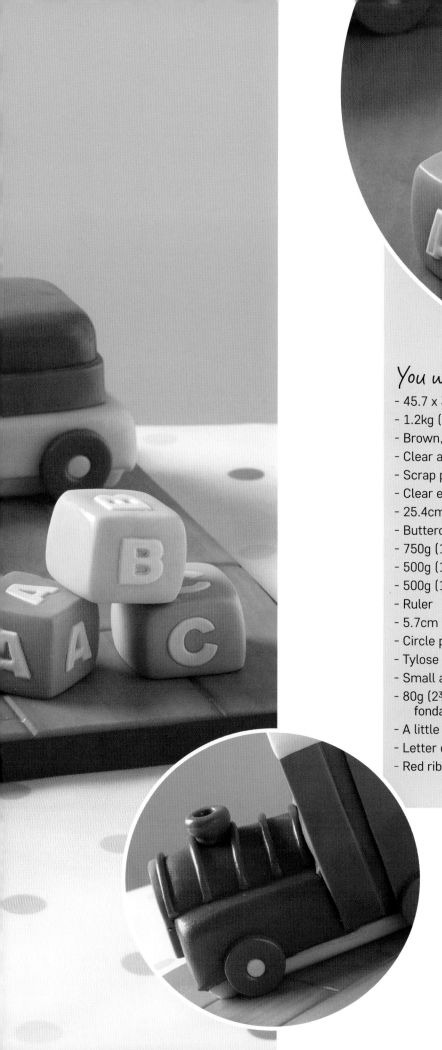

You will need

- 45.7 x 35.5cm (18 x 14in) rectangular cake drum
- 1.2kg (2lb 10oz) white fondant (sugarpaste)
- Brown, yellow and peach airbrush colours
- Clear alcohol such as vodka
- Scrap paper
- Clear edible spray glaze
- 25.4cm (10in) square madeira cake
- Buttercream
- 750g (1lb 10½oz) yellow fondant (sugarpaste)
- 500g (1lb 2oz) red fondant (sugarpaste)
- 500g (1lb 2oz) blue fondant (sugarpaste)
- Ruler
- 5.7cm (2¼in) and 3cm (1¼in) circle cutters
- Circle plunger cutters
- Tylose (CMC)
- Small amount of royal icing (see page 13)
- 80g (2¾oz) each of green and orange fondant (sugarpaste)
- A little white modelling paste
- Letter cutter
- Red ribbon and double-sided tape

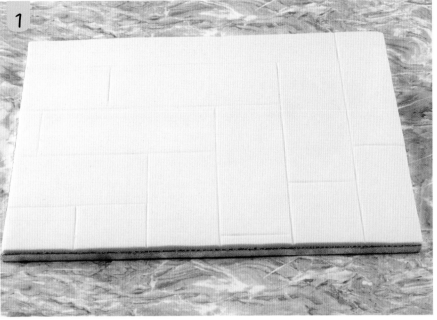

1 Cover the cake drum with white fondant (sugarpaste). Make a 20.3 x 7.5cm (8 x 3in) card template for a floor block. Score round the template with a Dresden tool as shown to make the floor pattern.

2 To create the effect of a knot in the wood, fill the airbrush bowl with brown, yellow and peach airbrush colour in the ratio 5:2:1, with 50% clear alcohol. Tear strips and knot shapes from paper. Hold a knot shape over the edge of the board and spray round it, then move it a little and spray round it again. Repeat to build up the effect.

3 To create the lined woodgrain, spray over the torn edge of a straighter piece of paper, moving and repeating as before. Change the direction of the strip according to the direction of the block, and keep changing the paper.

4 Add more brown to the mix and spray over the top of the woodgrain effect to deepen the colour. Spray into the grooves to darken them. Allow to dry and then glaze with clear edible spray glaze.

5 Cut the 25.4in (10in) square cake into four pieces, one 15 x 9cm (6 x 3½in), two 12.7 x 9cm (5 x 3½in) and one 7.5 x 9cm (3 x 3½in). All should be 5cm (2in) deep. Chamfer the bottom of all the pieces, cutting diagonally into the cake from 4cm (1½in) up down to the base.

6 Take the 15 x 9cm (6 x 3½in) piece to make the train engine. Place a 5.7cm (2¼in) circle cutter at the top of one end and score round it.

7 Mark 2cm (¾in) down from the top on either side of the circle.

8 Mark a faint line along the centre of the cake top lengthwise.

9 Put the small piece of cake on top at the back and mark the edge.

10 Cut into the side of the cake as marked in step 8, but ony as far back as the mark made in step 9. Repeat on the other side.

11 Carve round the curve of the engine on both sides to create the engine shape shown below.

12 Carve the curve at the top of the cab freehand.

13 To make the first wagon, take one of the 12.7 x 9cm (5 x 3½in) blocks of cake. Score a border 3.7cm (1½in) in from the edge and cut down 3.7cm (1½in).

14 Measure 3cm (1¼in) down on each side and score lightly all the way round. Put the knife in as shown, all the way through the cake but leaving 1.5cm (½in) at each corner uncut.

15 Lift out the central block as shown.

16 To make the second wagon, take the other 12.7 x 9cm (5 x 3½in) block of cake and use the offcut from step 15 as a template to create a border. Score round it as shown.

17   Score all the way round this block halfway up the sides, then cut in to a depth of 3.7cm (1½in) all the way round.

18   Cut off the border as shown.

19   Buttercream the engine and both wagons, including the chamfered lower edges. Take 100g (3½oz) of yellow fondant (sugarpaste) and roll it into a long sausage. Roll it flat to (1½in) wide and attach to the base of each part of the train. Tidy with a smoother.

20   Cover the first wagon with yellow fondant (sugarpaste). Roll out 400g (14oz) 5mm (¼in) thick and roughly 23 x 28cm (9 x 11in). Drape the piece over the wagon and push it into the shape. It doesn't matter if it splits in the middle because it will be covered. Make the edges as straight and square as possible using smoothers.

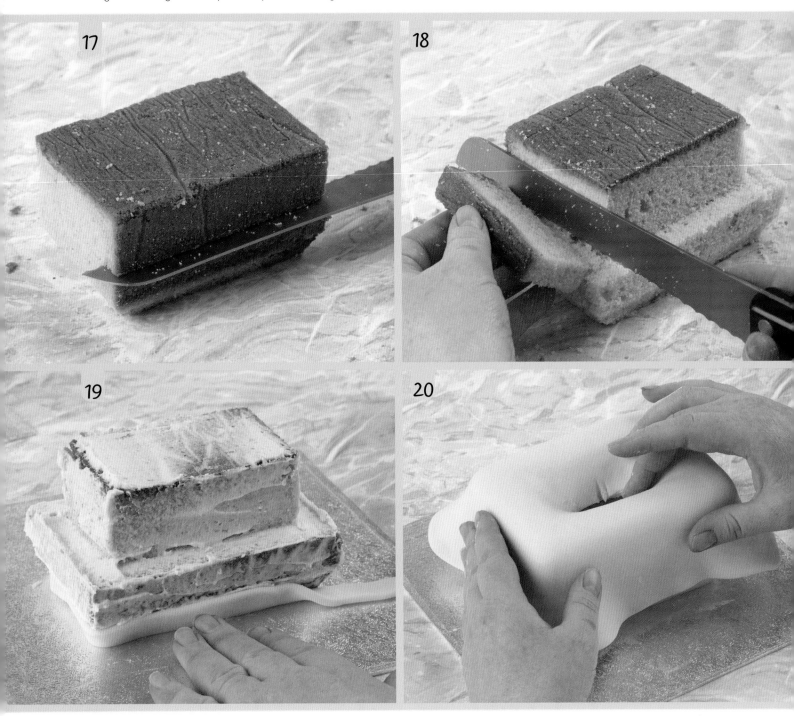

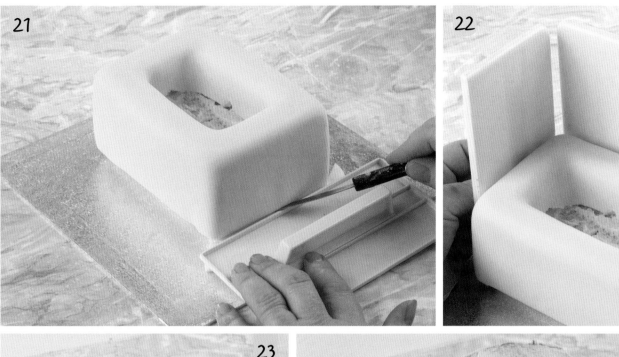

21 Use a smoother to get a straight line and trim at the bottom with the palette knife.

22 Sharpen the corners and the top with two smoothers.

23 Take 250g (8¾oz) of red fondant (sugarpaste), roll it out to approx. 15 x 20cm (6 x 8in) and cut one edge straight. Drape it over the front of the train's engine and shape it with your hands.

24 Use a smoother to accentuate the curves and trim as before.

25

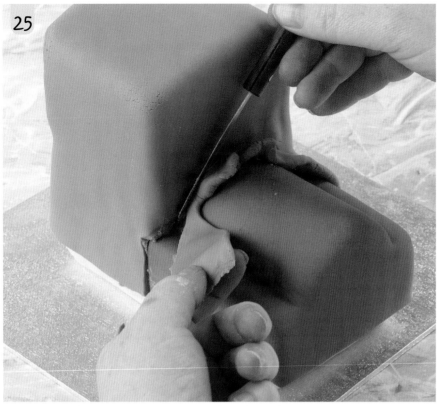

26

27

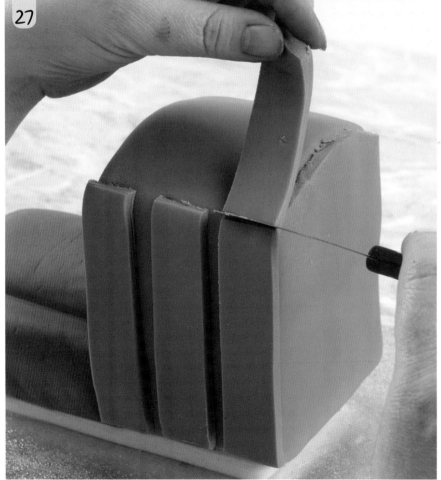

25 Take 370g (13oz) of blue fondant (sugarpaste) and roll out to approx.35.5 x 28cm (14 x 11in). Drape over the front and sides of the engine cab. Smooth with your hands and trim at the bottom and front.

26 Smooth and sharpen the edges with a smoother. Roll out 10 x 12.7cm (4 x 5in) for the back, stick on and trim as before.

27 Make six blue strips 2 x 11.5cm (¾ x 4½in). Use water to stick three to each side of the engine cab and trim neatly at the top.

28 Use a 5.7cm (2¼in) circle cutter to cut a circle from blue fondant (sugarpaste) and attach this to the front of the engine.

29 Make five long sausages of red fondant (sugarpaste) 3mm (⅛in) wide and 9cm (3½in) long. Place one at the back of the curved part of the engine to conceal the join, and one at the front, then space the others out evenly in between, to divide the engine into sections.

30 Make a funnel shape from a ball of blue fondant (sugarpaste). Hollow out the inside with a ball tool. Use water to stick the funnel to the second section of the engine.

31 Take 190g of yellow fondant (sugarpaste) and add Tylose (CMC) to make it stiffer. Roll out 6mm (¼in) thick and cut to 9 x 12cm (3½ x 4¾in) and place it on the roof of the engine cab. Straighten the edges with smoothers.

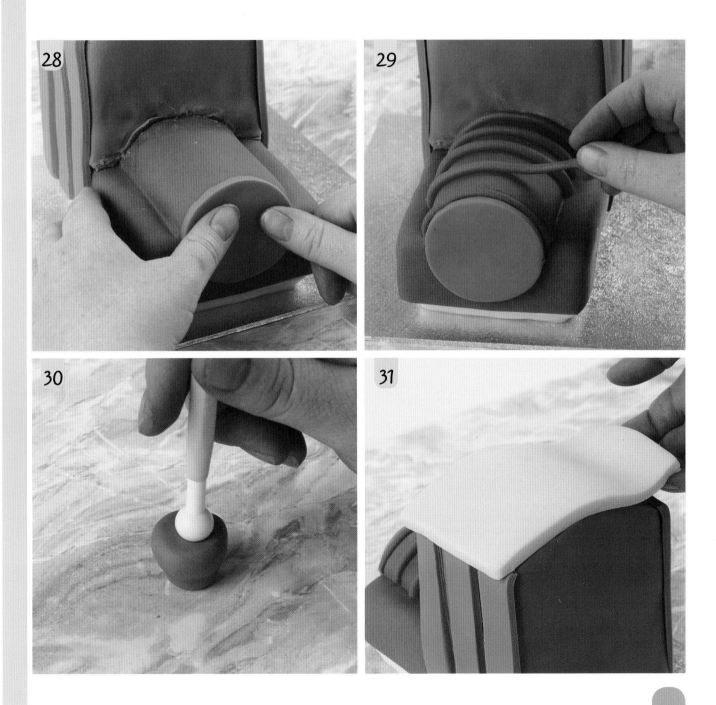

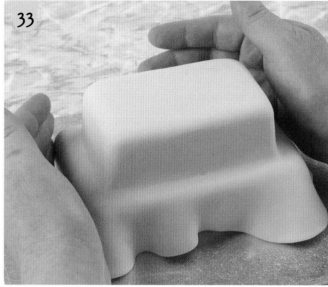

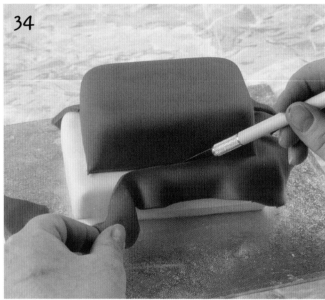

32 Use a 3cm (1¼in) circle cutter to cut the wheels from red fondant (sugarpaste) with added Tylose (CMC), rolled out 3mm (⅛in) thick. Roll out a little yellow fondant (sugarpaste), also with Tylose (CMC), to the same thickness. Use a medium circle plunger cutter to take out the centre of each wheel and replace it with a yellow circle.

33 Take 250g (8¾oz) of yellow fondant (sugarpaste), roll it out to 23 x 18cm (9 x 7in) and use it to cover the second wagon. Smooth it with your hands and a smoother.

34 Dampen the top yellow surface. Roll out 50g (1¾oz) of red fondant (sugarpaste) to 18 x 15cm (7 x 6in) and only 2mm (¹⁄₁₆in) thick. Cover the yellow top of the wagon, push in with the smoother edge and trim.

35 Roll out 60g (2oz) of blue fondant (sugarpaste) to a long strip and cut it to 2 x 38cm (¾ x 15in). Use water to stick it round the base of the red top.

36 Use royal icing to stick on the wheels, four on each part of the train. Make blocks to go in the first wagon from 100g (3½oz) each of red and blue fondant (sugarpaste), moulded into logs and further shaped with the smoother.

37 Make letter blocks from 80g (2¾oz) each of green, yellow and orange fondant (sugarpaste) with Tylose (CMC). Roll each into a ball and then shape into a cube using two smoothers. Roll out a little white modelling paste and use a letter cutter to create the letters. Stick these to the cubes using water.

38 Glaze the whole train with clear edible spray glaze. Arrange the train and blocks on the decorated cake drum. Trim the edges of the drum with red ribbon, using double-sided tape.

GET CRAFTY

This craft box would make a great cake for someone who loves sewing. Put in as much detail as you like – it is the realistic finish that makes it special. Use your imagination and adapt it into a jewellery or tool box.

You will need

- 40.6cm (16in) square cake drum
- 2.2kg (4lb 13½oz) white fondant (sugarpaste)
- Small coins
- Pink, black and brown airbrush colours
- 25.4 x 17.8cm (10 x 7in) madeira cake, 10cm (4in) deep
- 23cm (9in) square cake cards
- Buttercream
- Wide food-safe poly dowel
- 640g (1lb 4oz) white flowerpaste
- A little royal icing
- Ruler
- Tylose (CMC)
- Scrap paper
- Button and bead silicone moulds
- White vegetable fat
- Small amounts of modelling paste in various colours
- Clear edible spray glaze
- Edible paste colour in chestnut and cream
- 3.5cm (1³⁄₈in) circle cutter
- Circle plunger cutter set
- Edible lustre spray in silver, pink, pearl and black
- Black and blue edible pens
- Edible lace mix, mould and knife
- Fabric texture mat
- Cocktail stick
- Edible gold paint
- White ribbon and double-sided tape

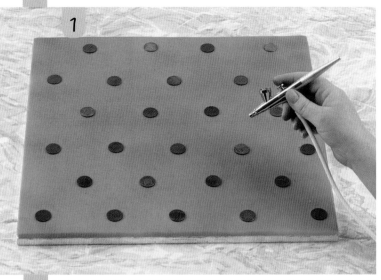

The finished effect.

1 Cover the cake drum with 1.3kg (2lb 14oz) white fondant (sugarpaste) and leave to dry. Place small coins at regular intervals as shown and airbrush pink. Remove the coins to reveal the pattern.

2 Level the cake at 9cm (3½in) high and trim 2.5cm (1in) off the width. Measure 5cm (2in) up from the bottom all the way round, score and then cut right through.

3 Cut a cake card to 22 x 7.5cm (8¾ x 3in). Place it on the bottom cake piece as a template to help you cut out the drawer space. Cut round the board, going back 6.5cm (2½in). Mark 2.5cm (1in) down the front of the cake piece.

4 Cut and take out the drawer piece.

5 Take a 23 x 14cm (9 x 5½in) cake card and buttercream the section you cut off the top of the cake to this.

6 Buttercream the drawer offcut to the smaller cake card you used as a template. Mark a 13mm (½in) border within the front and sides, and cut this out 13mm (½in) down from the top to create the inside of the drawer.

7 Take two pieces of wide food-safe poly dowel and trim to 5cm (2in) high. Push into the lower part of the craft box as shown.

8 Buttercream the top of the piece and the inside of the drawer, and place the top on, supported by the poly dowels.

9 Buttercream the whole piece, including the drawer. Take 100g (3½oz) of white fondant (sugarpaste) and roll it out to 25.4 x 15cm (10 x 6in). Stick this to the top of the craft box and trim it flush with the edges. The box needs really sharp edges, so use a smoother as a guide.

10 Take 400g (14oz) of white flowerpaste, roll it into a long sausage and cut two 25.4cm (10in) pieces and two 15cm (6in) pieces. Square the edges with a smoother to create prism shapes 2.5cm (1in) high and 2cm (¾in) thick. These pieces make the edges for the top tray of the craft box. Stick them in place using water, trim to fit and then cut diagonally to mitre the corners.

11 Cut diagonally across the corners of the shorter pieces and stick them on with water. Square with smoothers.

12 Make two pieces in the same way, 12cm (4¾in) long, and one piece 6.4cm (2½in) long, and stick these in place with water, as shown, to make the divisions in the tray.

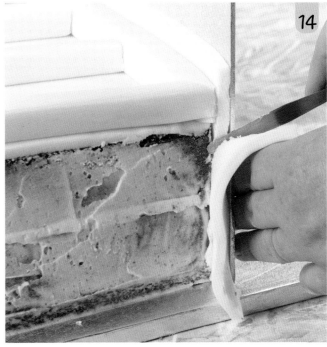

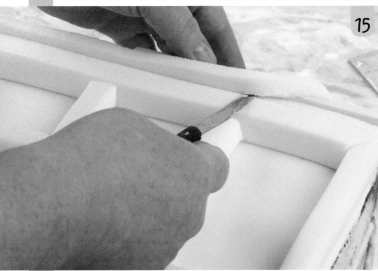

13 To cover the back of the craft box with fondant (sugarpaste), first brush water on the edge of the flowerpaste bar at the back. Roll out 900g (1lb 15¾oz) of fondant (sugarpaste) using plastic dowels to create an even depth, and cut to 12.7 x 26.6cm (5 x 10½in). Transfer onto a cake card and use this to lift the piece against the back of the box.

14 Smooth onto the back using smoothers and use the cake card as a guide to help you trim the edges neatly.

15 To trim the top, hold the piece in place with a smoother and use this as a guide to cut a straight edge. Smooth to hide the joins.

16 Cover the sides in the same way, with pieces 12.7 x 16.5cm (5 x 6½in). Cover the front in the same way as the back, then pierce through the hole for the drawer and ease the edges in neatly with your fingers, using the cake card above as a guide. Use a smoother to straighten.

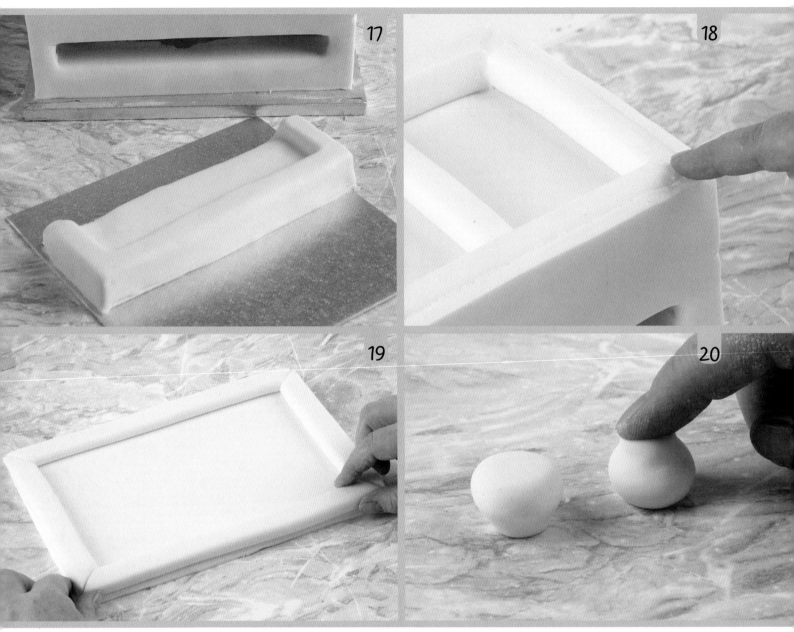

17 Roll out white fondant (sugarpaste) to 30.5 x 10cm (12 x 4in) and cover the drawer as shown. Smooth with your hands and use the smoother to get a straight, sharp finish, then trim.

19 To make the lid of the craft box, take a 25.4 x 16.5cm (10 x 6½in) cake card. Roll out 300g (10½oz) of white fondant (sugarpaste), drape over the board and use the smoother as a guide to trim the edges. Use 240g (8½oz) of white flowerpaste and make the edges of the lid in the same way as for the tray (see step 10), but only half as thick. Mitre the corners and stick the edges on with water. Use smoothers to straighten them and royal icing to conceal any gaps.

18 Repair any gaps in the box using a little royal icing. Apply it with a palette knife, wet it a little and smooth in with your finger.

20 Roll little balls of fondant (sugarpaste) mixed with Tylose (CMC), 2cm (¾in) across, then roll between your fingers to make a mushroom shape for the drawer knobs. Flatten a little against the work surface as shown.

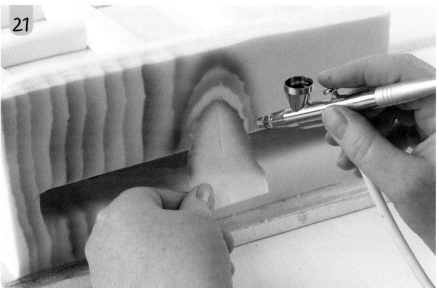

21 Create a woodgrain effect with the airbrush and 1:8 black to brown airbrush colour, making lines and knots as in the Toy Train project, steps 3 and 4 (pages 114–115). Give some panels a vertical and some a horizontal woodgrain. Spray the drawer and knobs as well. Allow to dry for twenty minutes.

22 Add more brown to the mix and add another coat over the whole piece. Allow to dry for twenty minutes.

23 Apply a deeper coat of just brown airbrush colour to add warmth.

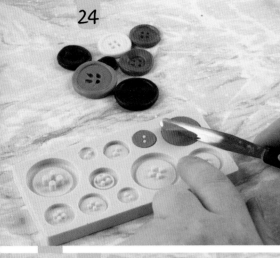

24

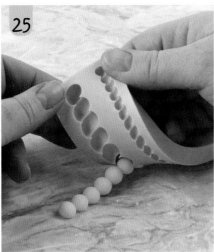

25

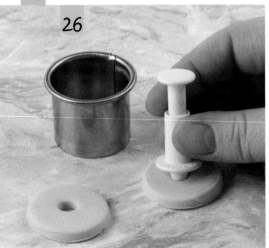

26

27

28

24 Take a small amount of modelling paste in various colours and press into a silicone button mould spread with a little white vegetable fat. Slice off the excess with a small palette knife to level it. Push out the buttons, allow to dry and then glaze with clear edible spray glaze.

25 Make a string of beads with white modelling paste, using a bead mould with a little white vegetable fat. Make a long sausage of modelling paste and press it into the mould. Cut off the excess paste as before, then push out the beads. You can spray them with pearl or silver edible lustre spray.

26 Make the tops and bottoms of the cotton reels with 90g (3oz) of fondant (sugarpaste) with Tylose (CMC) and coloured with chestnut and cream edible paste colour. Roll out and cut with a 3.5cm (1³/₈in) circle cutter, then use the smallest of the circle plunger cutters to cut out the middle.

27 Use 35g (1¼oz) of modelling paste in various colours to make six cotton reels. Roll short, thick sausages and use the smoother to press them down to 3.5cm (1½in) high. Texture with a palette knife to create the effect of cotton.

28 Stick on the tops and bottoms with a little water.

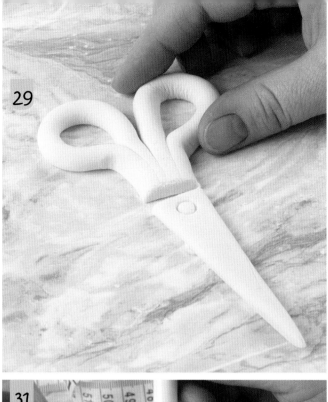

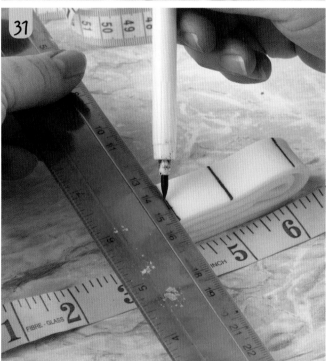

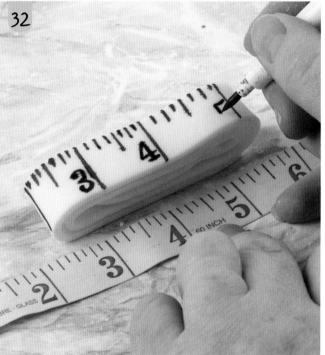

29 Take 12g (½oz) of white modelling paste. Roll one-third of it into a long cone and roll it flat, then sharpen it into the shape of the scissor blades using smoothers. Use a circle plunger cutter to indent the shape of the screw. Roll the rest of the paste into a long sausage and make two loops as shown for the scissor handles. Cut across the bottom, dampen with water and attach to the blades. Place on kitchen paper, spray with silver edible lustre spray, allow to dry and then glaze with clear edible spray glaze. Make two pairs of scissors.

31 Use black edible pen and a real tape measure as a guide to add the lines. Use a ruler to help you keep the lines straight.

30 To make the tape measures, take 20g (¾oz) of white modelling paste for each tape. Roll into a long sausage and then roll and trim into a flat 2cm (¾in) wide strip, 38cm (15in) long. Fold over as shown. Make two.

32 Add little lines and numbers.

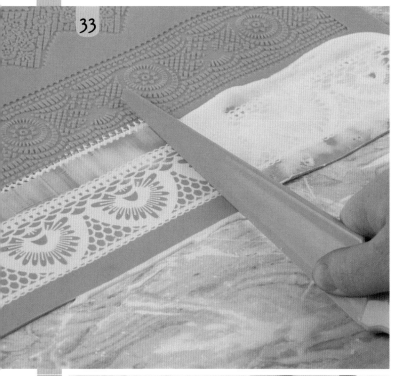

33 Make up the edible lace mix following the manufacturer's instructions. Paste the mix over the lace mould, making sure you fill all the sections. Scrape off the excess using the knife. Leave to dry overnight or bake in the oven, according to the manufacturer's instructions.

35 To make the wool, use fondant (sugarpaste) in a clay gun, choosing whichever colours you prefer.

34 When the edible lace is dry, peel it out of the mould. Spray the various sections of lace with edible lustre spray in different colours.

36 Make two pieces of fabric with180g (6¼oz) of modelling paste each in mint green and pink. Roll it out very thin, then place it over the fabric texture mat and use a small rolling pin to help transfer the pattern.

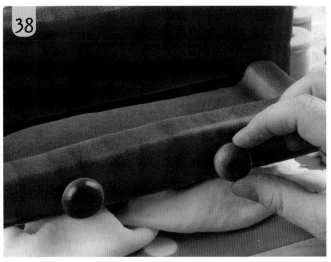

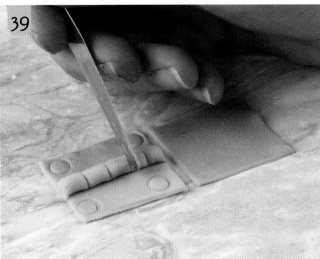

37 Place the cake on the decorated cake drum. Make supports for the drawer with two 2.5cm (1in) lengths of wide poly dowel covered in dampened modelling paste.

38 Arrange the fabric over the supports. Put the drawer in. Attach the knobs with bits of cocktail stick. Arrange the bits of lace in the drawer.

39 Lean the lid against the back of the craft box and attach it with royal icing. Make two hinges from rolled out modelling paste cut to 4 x 3cm (1½ x 1¼in). Impress the corners with a circle plunger cutter. Make a long sausage for the centre of each hinge, and score along it.

40 Stick the hinges in place with water and paint them with edible gold paint. Arrange all the items in and around the craft box. Trim the edge of the cake drum with white ribbon attached with double-sided tape.

TEMPLATES

The plectrum template for the Rock 'n' Roll project on page 46, shown full size.

The guitar body template for the Rock 'n' Roll project on page 46, shown half size. Enlarge to 200% before use.

The guitar head template for the Rock 'n' Roll project on page 46, shown full size.

The guitar frets template for the Rock 'n' Roll project on page 46, shown full size. You can use this or a real guitar as your guide for spacing the frets.

The guitar flame pattern template for the Rock 'n' Roll project on page 46, shown full size.

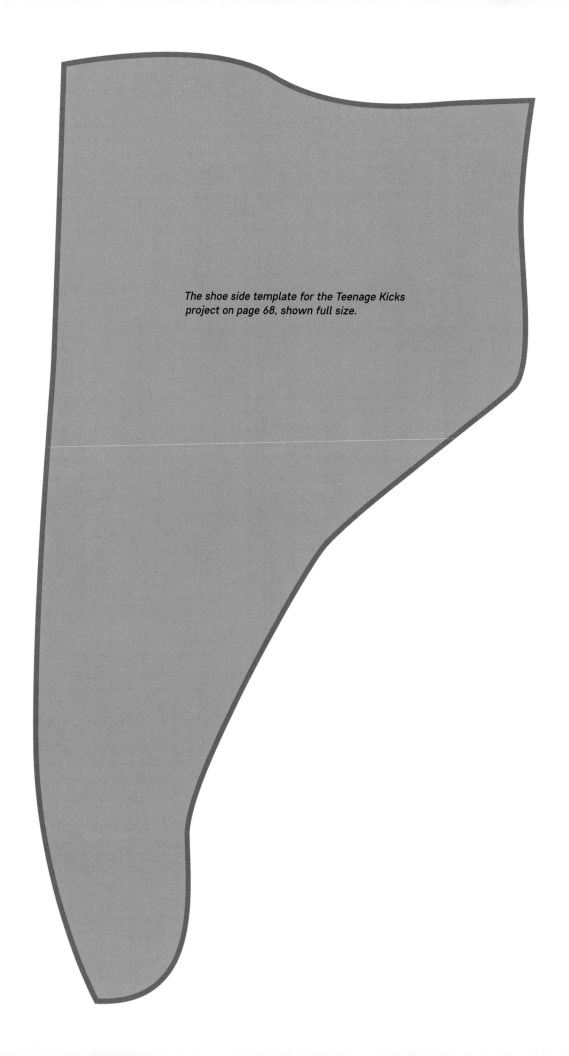

The shoe side template for the Teenage Kicks project on page 68, shown full size.

The shoe sole template for the Teenage Kicks project on page 68, shown full size.

The sunglasses and sunglasses arm templates for the Teenage Kicks project on page 68, shown full size.

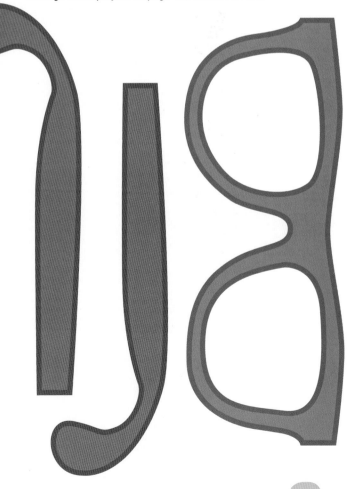

The basket template for the Catch of the Day project on page 78, shown full size.

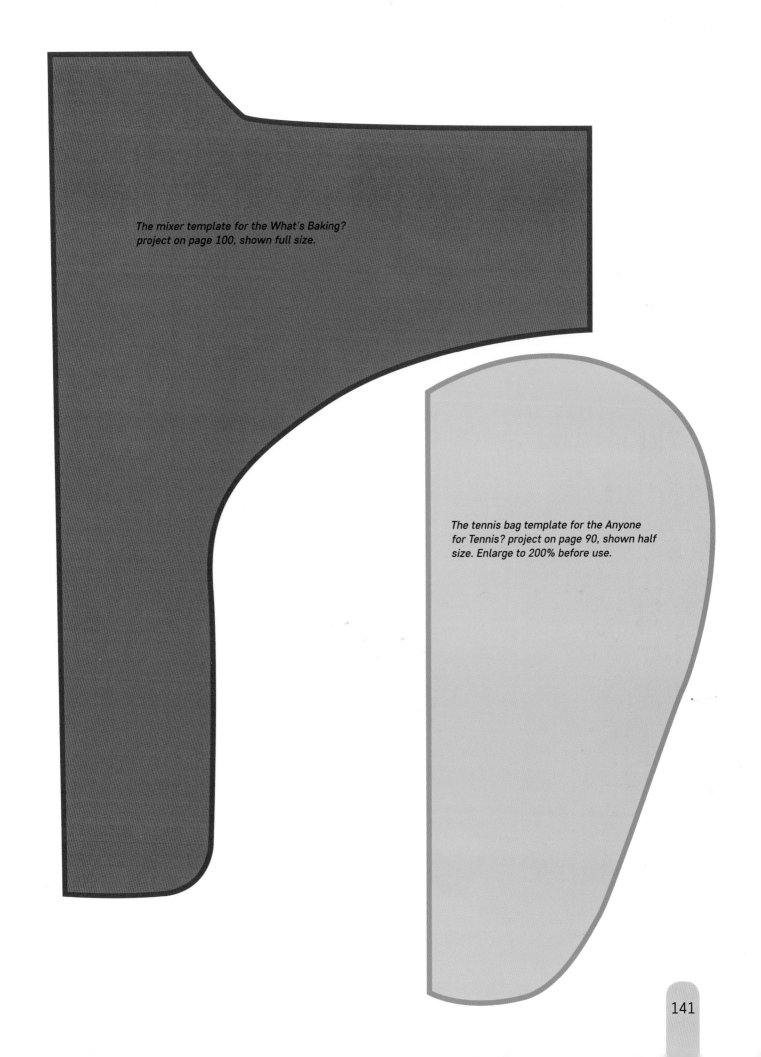

The mixer template for the What's Baking?
project on page 100, shown full size.

The tennis bag template for the Anyone
for Tennis? project on page 90, shown half
size. Enlarge to 200% before use.

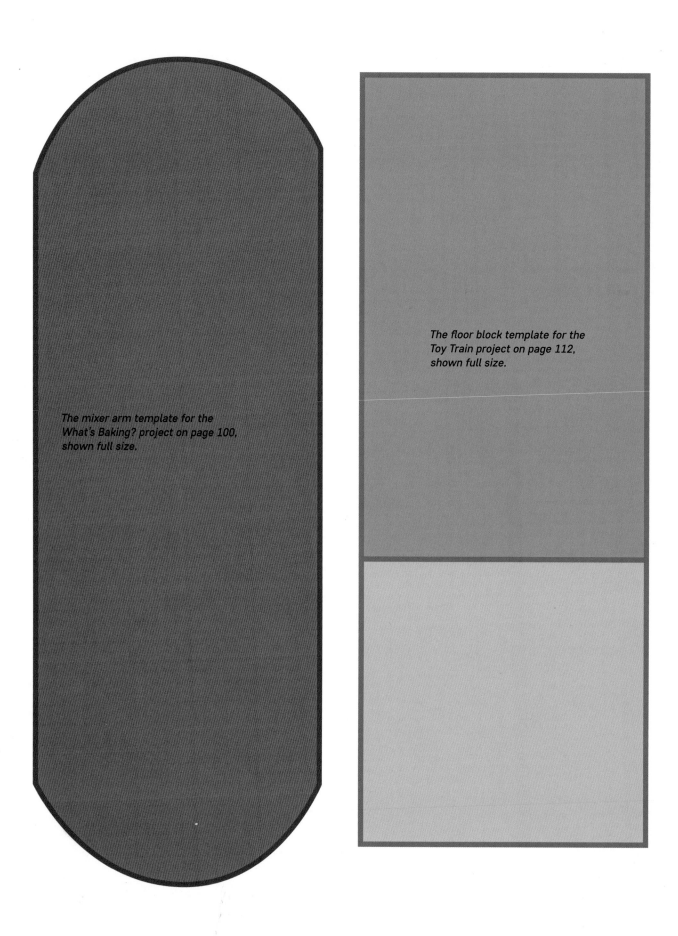

The mixer arm template for the
What's Baking? project on page 100,
shown full size.

The floor block template for the
Toy Train project on page 112,
shown full size.

INDEX

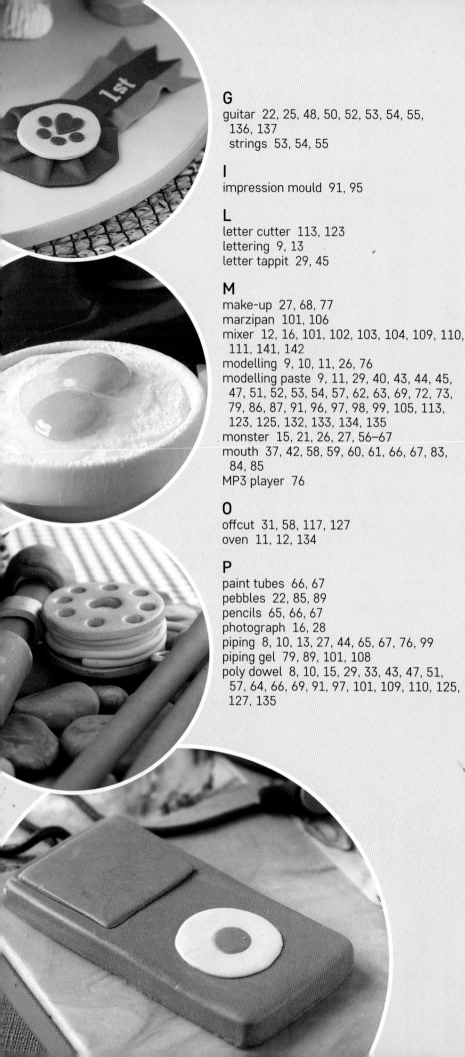